[redacted]

How to analyze your HANDWRITING

Manfred Lowengard

Golden Hands Books
Marshall Cavendish
London and New York

Credits

David Bailey/Sunday Times p 6. Chris Barker p. 16. Bettman Archive p. 31. Bodleian Library, Oxford p. 55. Camera Press p. 7. John Garrett pp. 60-61, 62. Keystone pp. 7, 14. Chris Lewis p. 5. Ben Manchipp MSIA p. 34. The Mansell Collection pp. 8, 13. National Portrait Gallery, London pp. 8, 9. David Newson p. 4. Pictorial Press p. 6. Popperfoto p. 14. Malcolm Scoular p. 43. Transworld Publishers p. 56. Warner Bros. p. 59. Dick Zimmerman p. 21.
Marion Richardson copy card on p. 9 from *Writing and Writing Patterns*, reproduced by permission of the University of London Press Ltd. Other school models reproduced from Blumenthal's *Schulschriften der Verschidenen Laender* by permission of Hans Huber Verlag, Berne. Samples of Sir Winston S. Churchill's handwriting on p. 9 reproduced by kind permission of C & T Publications Ltd. Other historical samples supplied by John Wilson and Mary Evans Picture Library.

Distributed in Canada by Thomas Allen and Son Limited,
850 York Mills Road, Don Mills 404, Ontario, Canada

Published by Marshall Cavendish Publications Limited,
58 Old Compton Street, London W1V 5PA

This material was first published by Marshall Cavendish Limited in *Handwriting: What it reveals about you* and *Come Alive.*

This volume first published 1975

Printed in Great Britain by
Ben Johnson and Company Ltd, York

ISBN 0 85685 105 1

Introduction

It may be a formal thank-you letter, a scribbled postcard, even a note to the milkman – but what does it really tell you about the writer? Dr Manfred Lowengard, a professional graphologist, shows how you can get a grasp of the fundamental rules of handwriting analysis and find out about yourself, your friends and acquaintances. For instance, you could help a teenager who is confused and shy – look at her handwriting to find out what she might be good at, and help her choose a career. Or a note from a new boyfriend – might it show something that doesn't usually come to the surface? Even a strange signature at the bottom of an official letter can tell you whether the writer is kind, timid, aggressive or sexy. Graphology is a recognized aid to psychology in many countries and a highly specialized subject. But you don't have to be a professor to analyze a sample if you follow the simple step-by-step method devised for this book. Many samples from well-known personalities or just ordinary people are included as well, to help you to get an insight into the character of a writer by combining your findings with some intuition and a lot of common sense.

Contents

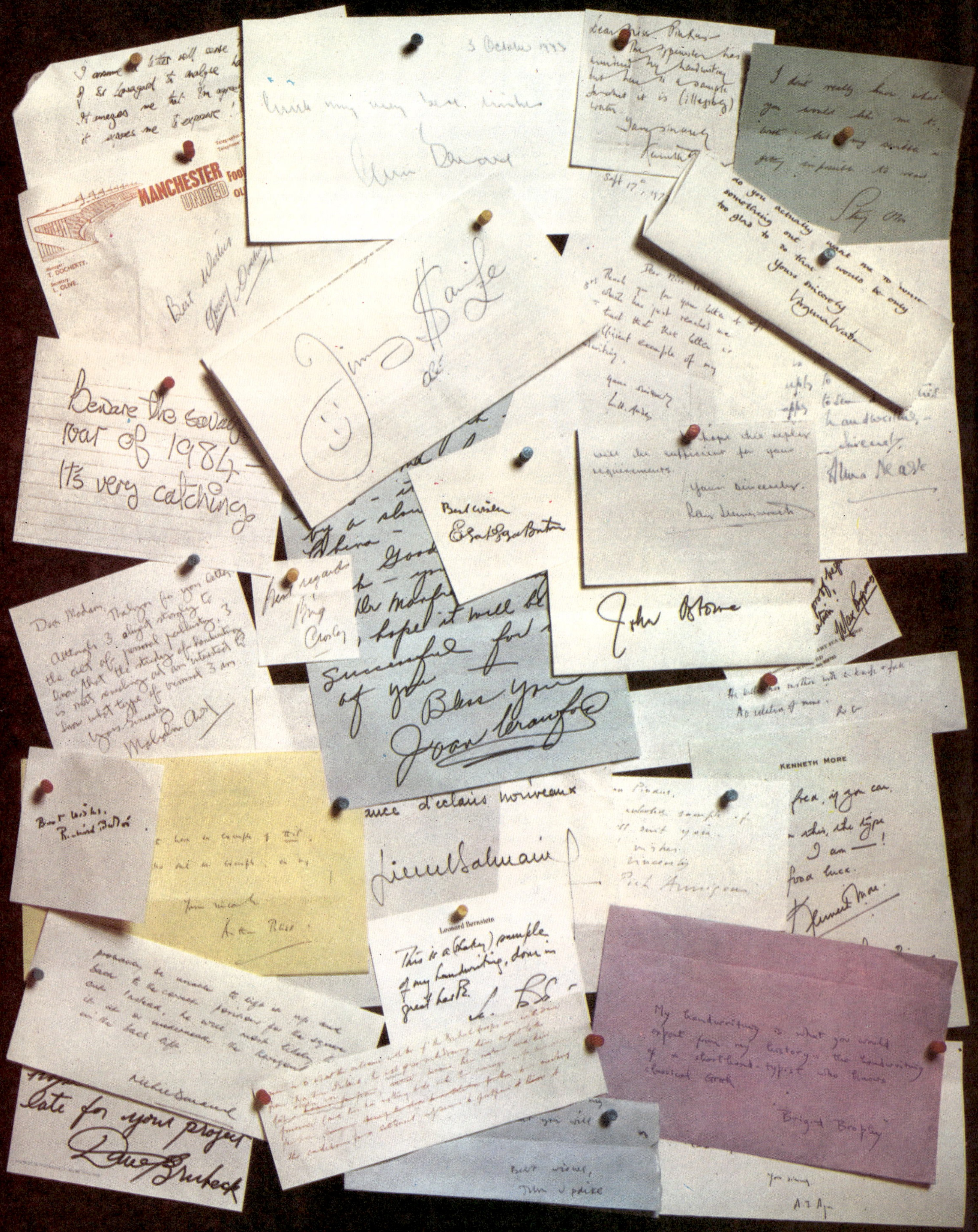
3 October 1973
MANCHESTER UNITED
Beware the savag
roar of 1984
It's very catching
Best regards
Bing
Crosby
Bless you
Joan Crawford
I hope this reply will be sufficient for your requirements.
Yours sincerely
KENNETH MORE
Leonard Bernstein
This is a (shaky) sample of my handwriting, done in great haste.
My handwriting is what you would expect from my history: the handwriting of a shorthand-typist who knows classical Greek
Brigid Brophy
Best wishes,
late for your project
Dave Brubeck

The meaning in writing

When you receive a letter, you probably cast an automatic glance at the writing on the envelope and instantly recognize whether the sender is a stranger or someone you know. Why is this so?

The answer is, of course, that everyone has his own individual way of writing. An American statistician has worked out that the possibility of finding two identical handwritings is 1:68 trillions, which is many times more than the population of our planet, to say nothing of the actual literate population.

What is writing?

Writing is a means of communication. Whether you look at Egyptian hieroglyphics, Nordic runes, Chinese characters, Gaelic scripts, Greek letters, Russian letters, or writings in our own alphabet, the marks are always for communication, to relay a message.

How does writing come into existence in the first place? Like all human activities, it has its first impulses in the brain, which sends the message through the arm to the hand of the writer. The hand is the most flexible extremity of the human frame and the most suitable to execute the art of writing. Experiments have shown, however, that when the pen is held between the toes, or even the lips, after a bit of practice people can write fluently,

Below: Letters, postcards, lists, bills . . . whatever you write is revealing.

CHRIS LEWIS

while maintaining their individual style. The term 'handwriting' is one of convenience. The activity could be called 'brainwriting'; but there's no need to be too pedantic here—the main point about writing is that it enables us to understand each other.

The origins of graphology

It was in 1875 that the learned Abbé Jean Hyppolite Michon first sat down to list the deviations from the 'school model' people learned to copy and, being an imaginative and intelligent man, he soon discovered that these variations from the norm were related to the writers' psychological make-up. The result was an early textbook which he called *Système de Graphologie*, with observations so penetrating that a slightly revised edition has been reissued quite recently.

How graphology can be useful

Graphology, the technical term for hand-writing analysis, is now part of the discipline of psychology, and can be studied at university level in almost every European country and in the United States. England is one of the few countries in Europe without a lecturer on the subject. Many people believe that the analysis of handwriting means prying into someone's personality and character without consent. This is misinterpreting the role of graphology. A professional graphologist must first have a working knowledge of psychology, as graphology is used as an additional aid by many psychologists. It should be his aim to interpret not only the facts he finds, but also the reasons and the underlying causes. He should try to find out why things are as they are. If you want to be a successful amateur graphologist, use your commonsense and your experience of people's feelings and emotions.

Everyone can learn the basic rules of handwriting analysis as they are set down here. The step-by-step analysis section has been arranged so that you can analyze any handwriting without previous knowledge. Combine a little thoughtful insight into people's problems with considerable understanding and you will have all the expertise you need.

There are many practical applications of the science of graphology, even for

Picture credits, left to right:
PICTORIAL PRESS;
DAVID BAILEY/SUNDAY TIMES;
CAMERA PRESS; CAMERA PRESS;
KEYSTONE

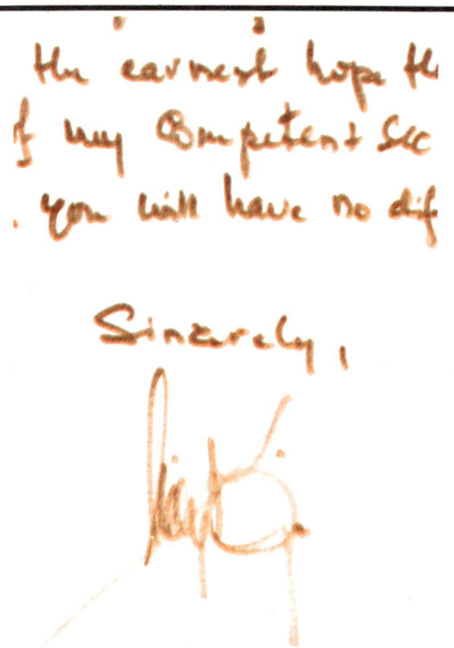
the earnest hope th
of my competent sec
you will have no dif

Sincerely,

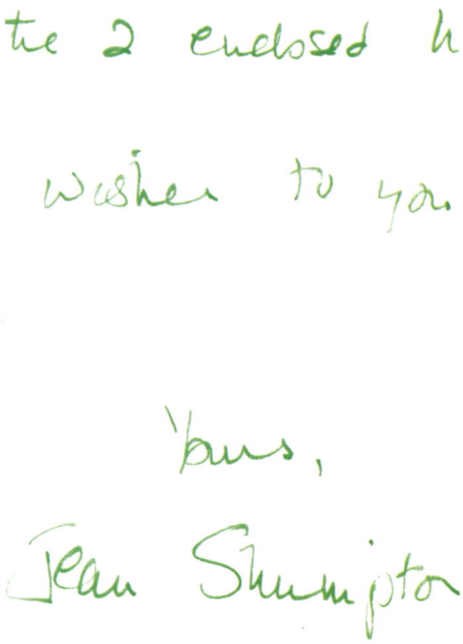
the 2 enclosed h

wishes to you.

Yours,

Jean Shrimpton

Victor Borge
The warm colour of the ink gives a welcome, and the clever letter formations indicate an intelligent and quick-witted man. The sharply placed i-dots, slightly to the right of the stem signify keen powers of observation.

The lines are extraordinarily straight, as are the margins. Here is a well organized and well mannered man who enjoys whatever he is doing. The large extensions into the upper zone, with their unusual loop formations, indicate a delightful imagination. This originality does not stop when it comes to his own assessment; the delicately curved line into the upper zone and the enormous circle of the 'o' indicate a certain self-deception in his personality. The long straight line slanting through the middle of the signature means that he can be obstinate if he does not get his own way.

Jean Shrimpton
This is a very natural writing. The letter formations are intelligent, and rather simplified than embellished, showing that she has retained her natural self. The lower zone loops show there is no hint of vanity, while the high t-bars indicate a refreshing degree of independence.

In spite of considerable speed, the i-dots and t-strokes are where they belong, and this shows that she has keen powers of observation and is very capable of adjusting herself to new surroundings or people or ways of life. The pressure of the writing is firm, and the spacing excellent, displaying organizing and planning abilities. Many final strokes are clipped, which indicate that she has suffered disappointments. The many garlanded connections indicate generosity almost to a fault. The small carefully closed a's and o's show she is not given to gossip and is a loyal friend.

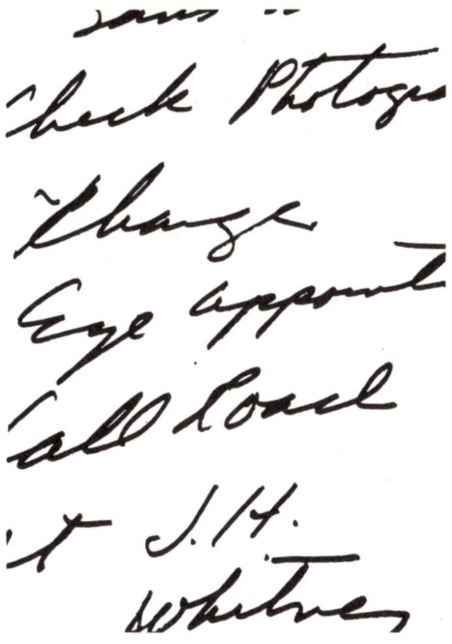

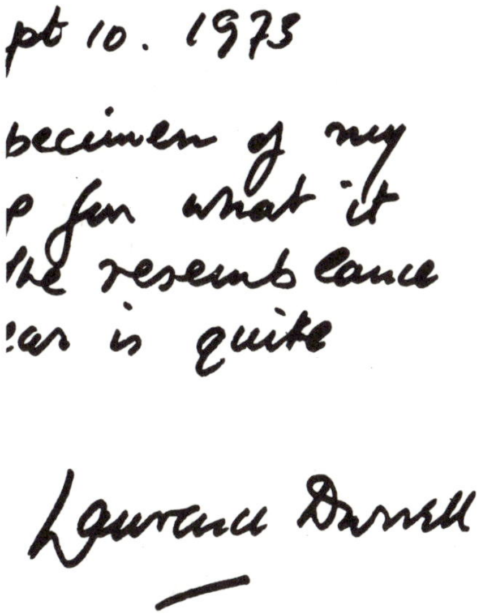

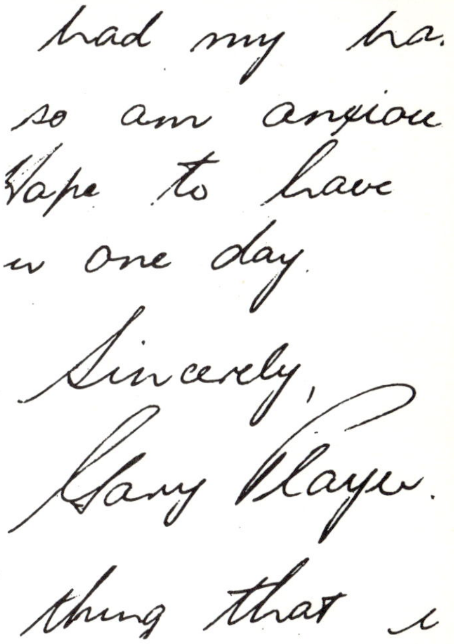

Art Buchwald
Full of vitality with lots of end-clippings. His ambitions have been curtailed and disappointed at times. The signature has no underlining and no full-stop at the end, which indicates self awareness. This well balanced personality is further expressed in the neat formation of the individual letters, and the ascending lines indicate a consequent optimism. The light pressure denotes artistry and a wicked sense of humour. The impression is that he does not like the reality he has to face and that he tries to transform it into something nicer.

Lawrence Durrell
The felt-tipped pen gives the writing a warmth which it otherwise would lack, because this is a rather sharp script. It is fast, it is legible, and the lines are ascending. The connections vary, thereby achieving the fastest route of progress. There is, however, a syllable-impulse rather than a word-impulse, pointing to a man who thinks before he acts. The lower and middle zones are emphasized, indicating not only sincerity, modesty but also a love of good things. The overall roundness specifies good-naturedness and a feeling for humanity. The open 'a's' and 'o's', together with the underlining of the signature, show us a man who is not afraid to speak the truth and who can thus be trusted.

Gary Player
This large, neat, legible script shows an exacting, precise man who does nothing without careful consideration. The predominant upper zone and firm pressure indicate that he thoroughly enjoys positive action. His round, almost school-model hand means he is kind, but no fool either. This is confirmed by the absence of end-garlands and the firm, down-stroke word endings. The firm t-bars indicate good powers of observation. This is the writing of a man who uses his considerable common sense to sum things up.
The whole script has an unassuming air. The upper zone formations imply ambition, and the capitals in his signature indicate personal pride. But nothing is overdone. He is happy with his status in society and a very slight wavyness in his otherwise straight lines show a sensitivity he does not show in public.

the amateur. From a quick study of the writing of a friend, you can discover traits in his personality which will lead you to greater understanding and compassion. Clues to the make-up of an applicant for a job can be gained from a sample of his handwriting. Is he reliable and conscientious? A hard worker? Has he managerial potential? Is he frank or secretive?

The psychiatrist or psychologist who does a quick graphological study can find immediate clues to the personality of a patient which he will want to pursue, saving hours delving for subconscious traits of which the analyst is unaware. Marriage guidance counsellors can help couples by looking at samples of writing from each.

Some professional graphologists even claim to be able to detect physical ailments such as poor circulation, heart disease or digestive disorders. For instance, heart disease can show itself in fraying line formations in the upper part of letters. You will probably need a magnifying glass to see them clearly. However as often as not, these are signs of fatigue—and you will probably be able to tell from other signs in the writing whether the writer is the sort of person who would overwork or stay up late every night at discos and parties!

Signs of illness can often be detected long before the writer is aware of them himself, so handwriting analysis can act as a useful early warning system. Of course, a graphologist would never attempt a diagnosis, but would certainly suggest a visit to the doctor for a check up.

Only adults have a fully developed writing but less experienced writings do point out developing personality trends. Teachers find handwriting analysis helpful in detecting and following the development of intellect and personality in children, particularly in overcrowded classrooms where truly individual attention to each child is impossible. Handwriting analysis is particularly useful in adolescence when vocational guidance is needed but the child has not yet shown in which direction his potential lies.

A toddler not yet of school age copies letters from posters or television and forms his own delightful variations. Even if he only draws pictures, the way he uses the drawing paper and the themes he picks provide clues about his evolving psyche to concerned and objective parents.

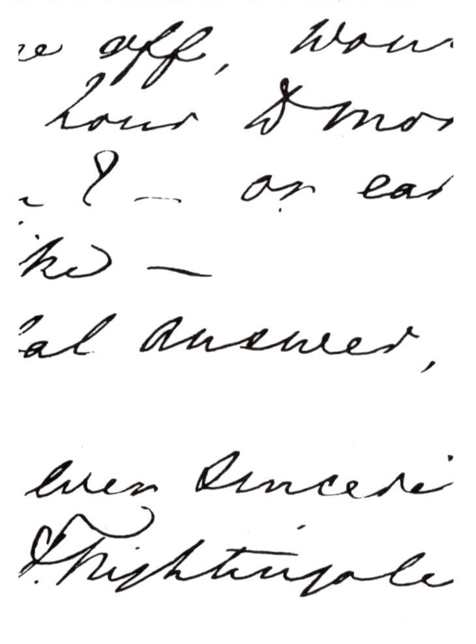

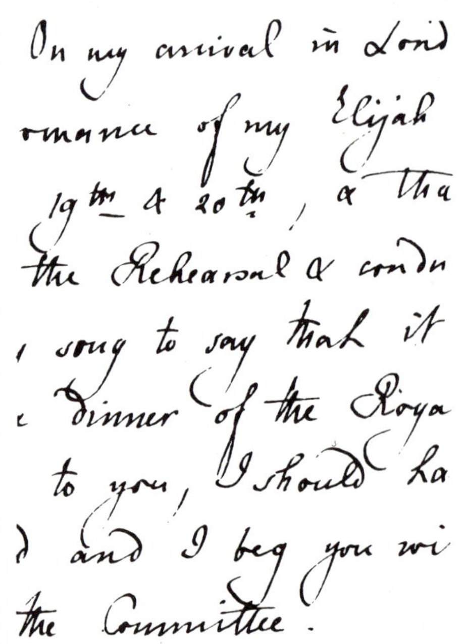

Florence Nightingale
The delightful flourish of the letter 'F' in the signature gives away the gentle sweetness of this intelligent and determined personality; it hooks to the spiritual sphere and anchors soundly to the down-stroke, showing her earthiness and realism. All letter-formations are original without being distorted or illegible; and the straightness of the lines, combined with the firm pressure, show the determination and energy she put into her plans. All three zones are well formed, and when simplification was possible, she took the shortest route. There was no unnecessary delay, false politeness or idle chatter in her, but a will to succeed and a superior ability to organize and get things done. The end-garlands show her sincere desire to help. This letter could have been written today, so modern and contemporary does it look.

Mendelssohn
Considering that this writing is over 150 years old, it looks extraordinarily contemporary. A neat writing, executed with delicate pressure using a writing instrument infinitely more difficult to control than our ball-pens, shows the depth of his feelings and the fluctuating middle zone in the notes shows his sensitivity. The end-garlands tell how gentle and warm-hearted he must have been. The rhythm and the upright style of the writing and the rhythmical distribution of pressure indicate a healthy control of his emotions.

Open 'a's and 'o's show his frankness and openness with just a hint of tactlessness. The firmness of the underlining of his signature shows that he knew what he wanted, and the originality of his letter formations indicate that he was intellectually advanced.

Picture credits, left to right:
NATIONAL PORTRAIT GALLERY, LONDON (detail) THE MANSELL COLLECTION NATIONAL PORTRAIT GALLERY (detail) NATIONAL PORTRAIT GALLERY (detail) NATIONAL PORTRAIT GALLERY (detail)

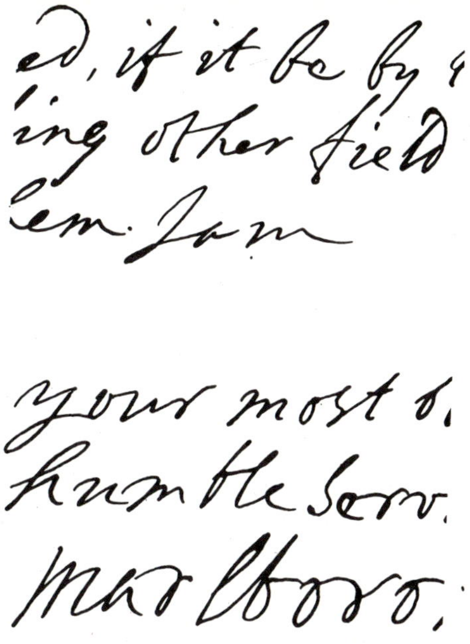

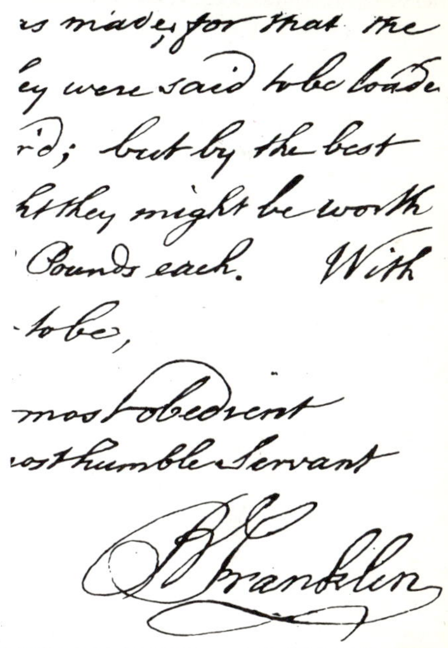

Dr. Samuel Johnson
This sample, written with a quill, shows energy and intelligence. Some letter formations—'I', 'D', 'M'—show good flow, speed, and intelligent simplification which increases the speed without impairing legibility. Any lack of legibility is due to bad ink flow. The upright script, with letters going straight from upper to lower zone, indicates a methodical way of thinking and working. Wit, if not sarcasm, and absolute frankness are shown in the open 'a's and 'o's and the sharp pressure. I-dots are exact or slightly ahead and accentuated, confirming a far-sighted wit and critical ability. Distribution is clear with a decreasing left-hand margin—an attempt to control the generosity exhibited in the frequent end-garlands. Arcades in the upper zone show respect for tradition and convention.

The Duke of Marlborough
A very speedy writing, large and rich in pressure. The word connections are poor, and occasionally he tries to connect letters by a kind of welding method. Letter formations are delicate. The 'd' in particular shows culture, intelligence and interest and pleasure in beautiful things, whilst ink-filled loops in the lower zone confirm his sensuality and love of beauty. The name is larger than the rest of the script—he was aware of his status and of his abilities. However note that there is no underlining and no full-stop at the end of his signature. In a large writing, this indicates that he was open to advice, and in this respect was indeed the "humble servant", he calls himself. The i-dots are exactly placed, and occasionally ahead of their stems, suggesting good powers of observation, a keen memory and a speedy reaction to stimuli.

Benjamin Franklin
Here we have delightfully old-fashioned American writing. Every movement and line is carefully and deliberately designed and formed. The writing proceeds in straight lines to and from straight margins, on both sides. The even rhythm ends with the final flourish of the signature. The many leftward movements and arcades show intense loyalty to tradition. His manual skill is shown in the simple letter formations which he has delicately transformed into pieces of illustrative art. The exact, slightly high i-dots indicate fine powers of observation and a good factual memory. This is the writing of a diversified craftsman, absolutely sincere and honest. The large, slightly enriched signature shows pride and vanity, but this is overshadowed by the good rhythm, pressure and general layout.

Learning to write

Everybody learns to write at school by copying from a book or from the shapes the teacher puts on the blackboard. Every child eventually develops his own style, thereby forming a writing which is uniquely his own, but the letters will follow the general pattern of his school model. In the English-speaking countries, even though the basic alphabet is the same, this school model is subtly different, as the illustrations show.

This is why a graphologist always asks for the nationality of the writer under analysis. He need not actually read the text of the writing he analyzes, but, since graphology assesses the deviation from the norm, it is essential to know the origin of the school model. This is especially true in analyzing a passage written in a language other than that of the original school model. For example, a Swedish national makes i-dots like little circles, as in his school model. This feature has a quite different interpretation if it is used by a writer educated in Britain.

Generally, the size of the school model is relative to the country it represents. Australian writing is a little larger than English writing. The handwriting of Swiss people is smaller. But psychology can also come into play and some inhabitants of a small country will write a very large hand, as if trying to compensate for a kind of national inferiority complex. Since English is spoken and written all over the world, and a writing style is as difficult to lose as a spoken accent, it is necessary to study the various school models. When odd letter formations appear, they must be compared to the school model of the country where the subject learned to write.

Below: Ten-year-old Lee has already formed his own unique style of writing.

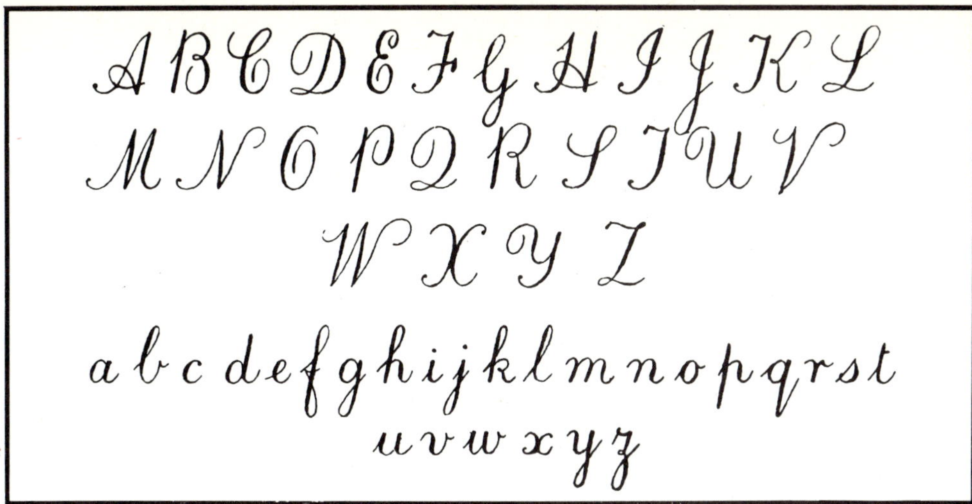

Australia The size is large, as is the country itself. Pressure is good, the loops are full, and the capitals are more elaborate. The writing is well connected, and the d's and t's are smaller than the other letters of the upper zone. T-bars are on the right of the stems, and do not cross them.

New Zealand's school model (not shown) leans forward to a much greater degree than the Australian one (about 70°). The p's and q's are shorter than other lower zone letters. A variety of shapes exist for capitals.

England This school model gives a slow, rhythmic script with garlanded connections and a large middle zone. It is mostly upright, but has a slight forward leaning trend. Pressure is firm and unexaggerated, and the words are well connected. The t's are lower than other upper zone letters. Nowadays small children are taught to print first, not usually connecting the letters until 7 or 8 years. Many schools teach italic script at a later stage, which includes careful thick and thin strokes and angular connections.

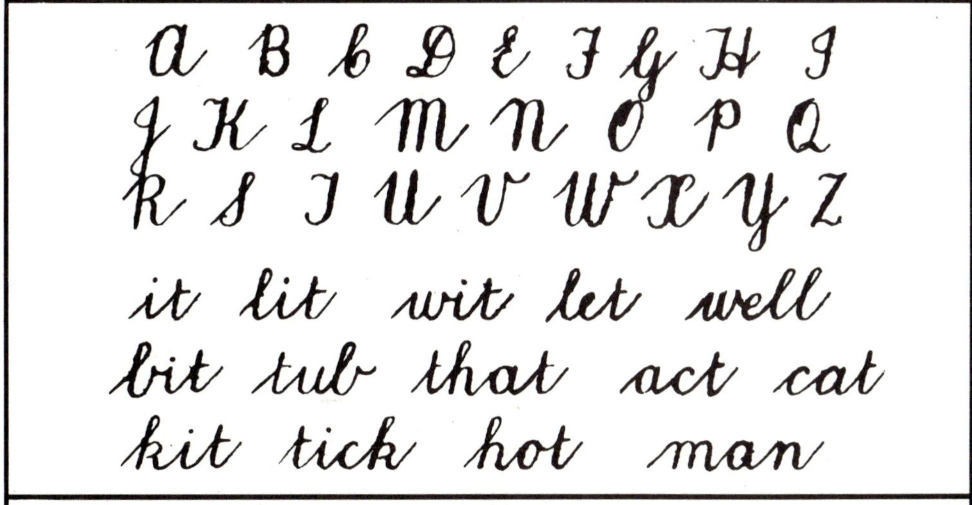

South Africa The school model shows heavy pressure. It is comparatively narrow, but leans forward a little. The capitals are slightly embellished, and the writing well connected. The bars are to the right of the stem, not crossing it, and the t's and d's are slightly smaller than other letters in the upper zone. First and last letters have long flourishes.

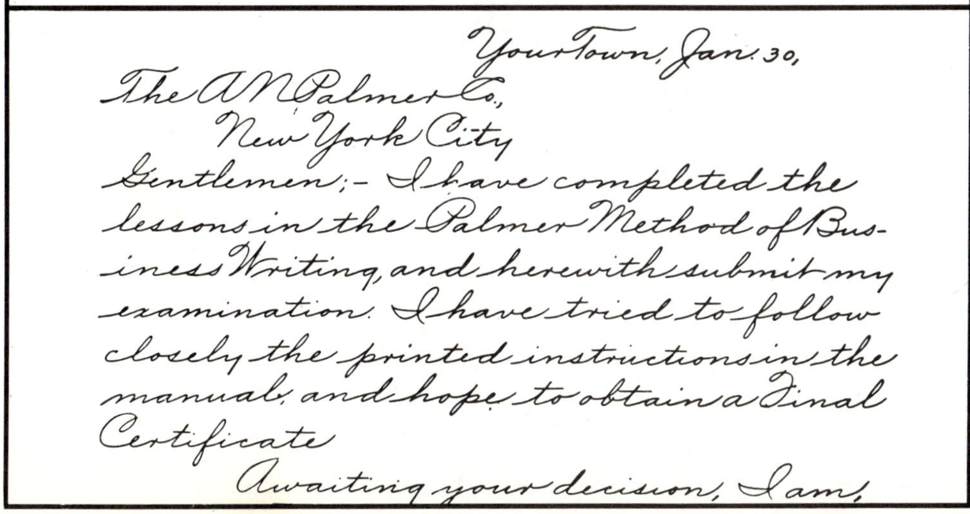

The United States and Canada This model shows a marked lack of pressure. The lower zone is large. The writing leans forward, the formations are simple, the loops are large, and the writing is well connected. The capitals are, in spite of being somewhat simple, enriched or embellished. The first and last strokes are large and often curved. Models vary from state to state, but retain the same fundamental characteristics.

These children are learning how to write. If they have any problems which they are unable to communicate, a trained graphologist could probably detect them.

How you write

The way we write is determined by three impulses—'motor', 'formative' and 'spatial'—all of which stem from the brain. Though writing may change superficially according to mood or method (the writing you use for a formal letter probably seems very different from a scribbled shopping list), the fundamental characteristics are the same.

The motor impulse

When you need to write, a message is sent from the brain to the muscles of the hand. It is therefore easy to understand that the graphologist talks of the 'motor impulse' as the basis of all writing. All that is needed for it to operate is an able-bodied human being with normal reflexes, reasonably good eyesight and a memory for the shapes of the alphabet used as means of communication.

The formative impulse

With the 'formative impulse', we can actually begin to analyze writing because this second impulse is the result of the writer's individuality and makes writing differ from the school model. As a result, the letters are shaped in a fashion entirely of each person's own making and design.

The spatial impulse

People write on a variety of surfaces: paper, cards, blackboards—even walls—and it is significant to note how writing is organized according to the space available. This is known as the 'spatial impulse'. The formation of lines and margins play an important part in handwriting analyses.

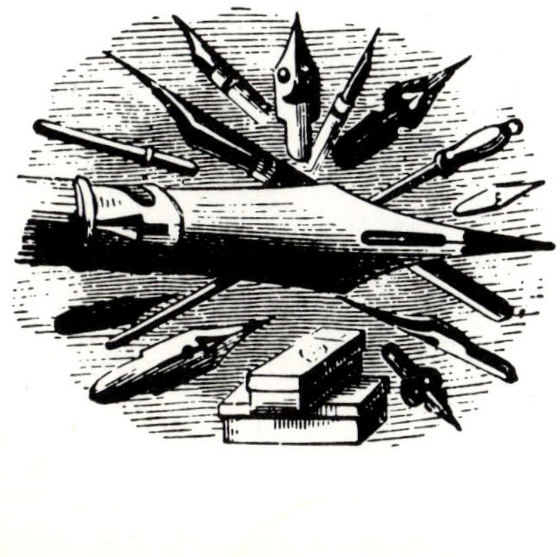

Left-handed writing

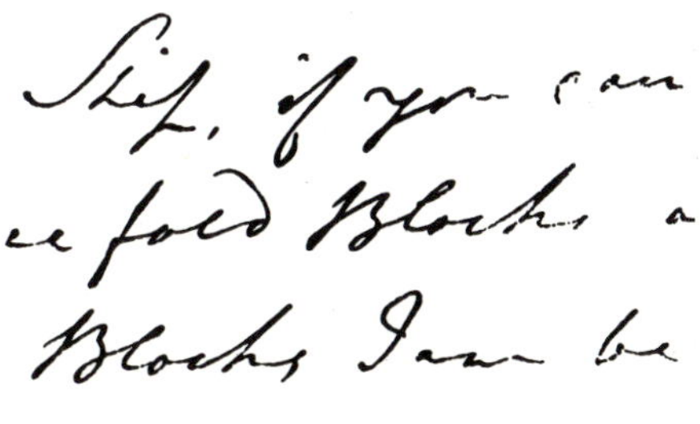

THE MANSELL COLLECTION

Lord Nelson, who was naturally right-handed, taught himself to write with his left hand after he lost his right arm in a battle. Compare the two here: top, his right-hand script; bottom, left-handed.

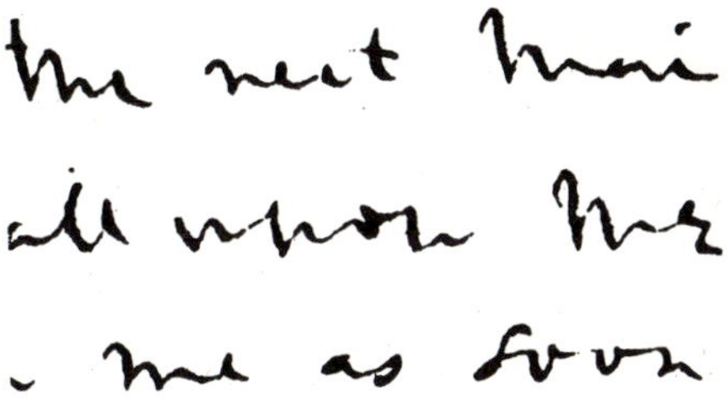

It is not as easy as it may seem to find out if a writer is left-handed. People seem to believe that left-handed writing must slant to the left. In fact this is rarely the case. Here the use of an orange stick or toothpick is very handy. Take the instrument and try to copy the way the letters were formed. If you find the task awkward with the right hand, try to use your left one. Very often you will find that the movement comes more naturally.

Left-handedness is not important to the graphologist, since it gives no indication as to the writer's character or personality. However, until quite recently, children who were left-handed by nature were often forced to use their right hands, and this sometimes resulted in a nervous disturbance. Nowadays, left-handedness is considered quite natural—merely rarer than right-handedness. Needless to say, among left-handers there are as many shades or degrees of intelligence, decency, honesty and so on as there are among right-handers, and the same rules of graphology apply to both.

Does writing change with age?

Since handwriting reflects the writer's state of mind and the degree of wisdom acquired by living, making mistakes and coping with difficult situations, it would be strange if signs of psychological development did not appear in the writing as well. If you look at a letter written by a child or teenager and compare it with one written by the same person in mature age, you are bound to find marked differences. These differences depend not only on the manual skill and dexterity developed over the years, but even more on the degree of adaptability that the writer has acquired. Everyone has moments of happiness, times of despair and disaster or emotional upsets. We are all forced to make decisions which may affect the rest of our lives. If people fail to respond to such challenges in a positive manner, if they try to avoid responsibility out of laziness, their lives are bound to develop quite differently from the way they would had they accepted all challenges as natural and positive forces.

Writing can reflect changes like these over a lifetime, and it is interesting to see if potentials seen in adolescent handwriting are reflected in the same person's writing in later life.

Some psychiatrists use the information derived from handwriting from many different periods of a patient's life for diagnosis and consequent treatment, watching, of course, to see if their patients' writing improves as treatment proceeds.

Sir Winston Churchill's writing in public life

1910
At this time, Churchill was already Home Secretary, having 'crossed the floor' to join the Liberal Party.
This well-spaced and well-shaped script, showing many Greek 'e' formations, indicates leadership and clear thinking. Pressure is strong, becoming a little smudgy in places, which may indicate that enjoyment of the good things in life was always present at this period of his life. At the same time the simplicity of letter formations and the neat connections show that the writer was capable of adjusting himself to circumstances.

POPPERFOTO

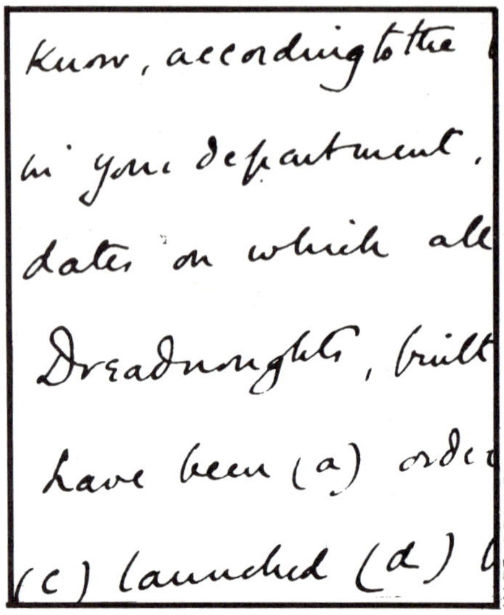
know, according to the
in your department,
dates on which all
Dreadnoughts, built
have been (a) orde
(c) launched (d)

KATE GRILLET

1936
Churchill was now a vociferous Conservative backbencher — bitterly opposed to the official policy of appeasement.
The writing is faster, and in a way more simplified, which means, of course, that concentration on essentials was greatly increased. The dagger-like 't'-stroke, placed on top of the letter, indicates his directness, and since the degree of connection is very good indeed, probably this was a time of forceful argument and discussion. Again, one does not find a trace of vanity, but only determination to get things done.

KEYSTONE

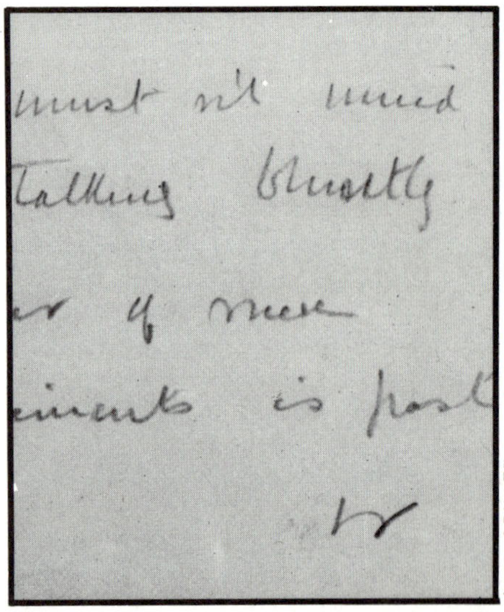
must not mind
talking bluntly
of of mere
iments is post

KATE GRILLET

1946
After the triumphs of the Second World War, Churchill and his party were voted out of office. During this year he made a famous speech in which he coined for the first time the phrase, 'the Iron Curtain'.
This writing is much smaller. This is mainly due to the fact that concentration on essentials had increased, and wisdom and experience ruled his thoughts and actions. The increased pressure indicates how successfully he coped with slight physical fatigue, shown in some cracks in his down-strokes.

KEYSTONE

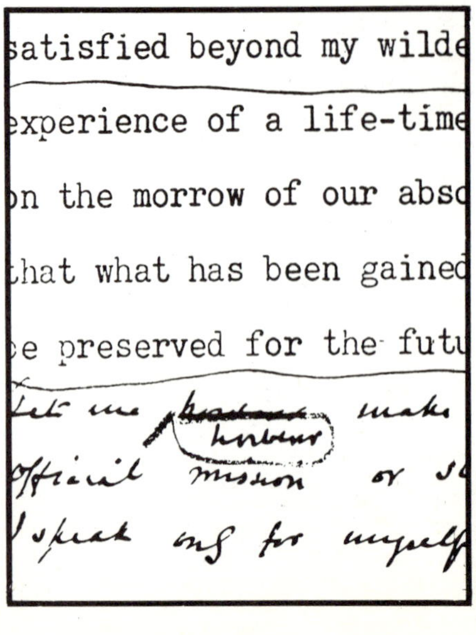
satisfied beyond my wilde
experience of a life-time
on the morrow of our abso
that what has been gained
be preserved for the futu
Let me however make
official mission or s
I speak only for myself

KATE GRILLET

The three zones

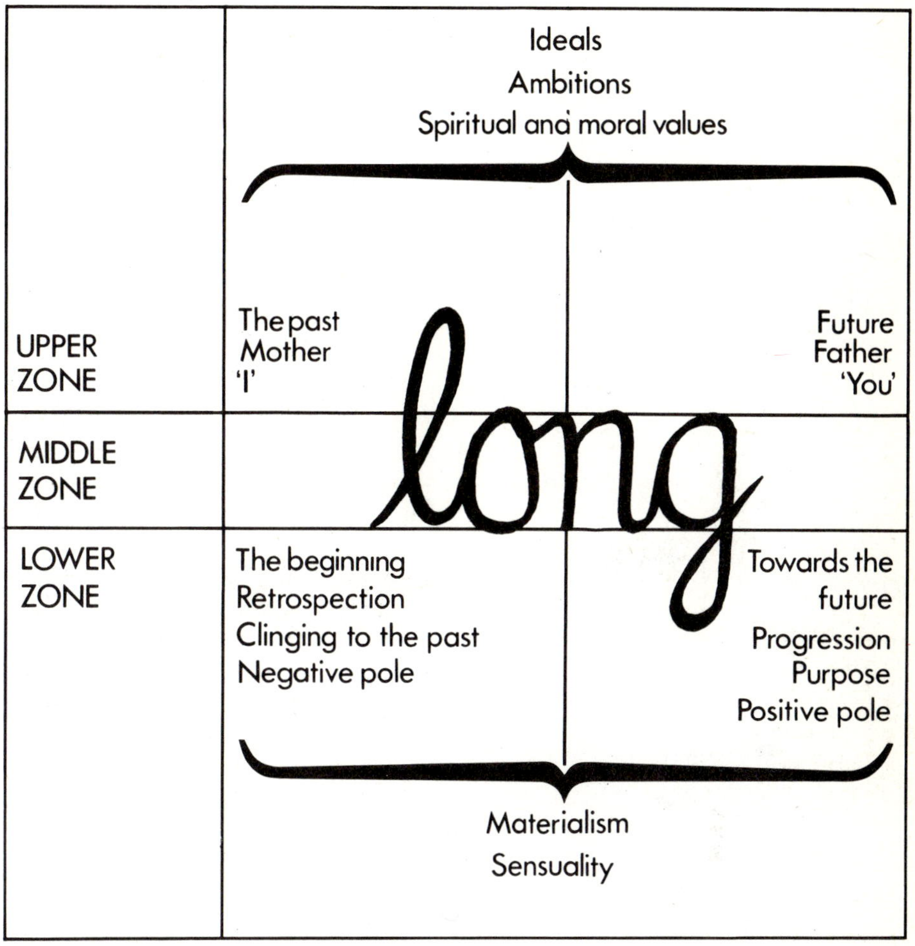

The three zones
The alphabet consists of two kinds of letters: capitals and small letters, or in graphological jargon: Majuscles and Minuscles. They represent the foundation of all writing.
The diagram shows that letters can be divided into three 'zones'—the upper, middle and lower. These three zones are the most important part in graphology, for they provide the cornerstone of the whole analysis. If you follow the way the pen moves over the surface during the act of writing, you will find that it is a constant movement from the top to the bottom of the line, and at the same time from the left towards the right. It also will become obvious that all movement entering the lower zone is directed more or less towards the writer while movement up into the upper zone goes away from it.

The meaning of the zones
The English language speaks of people who 'get *down* to business', or 'live *up* to ideals'. This division is also seen in graphological analysis.
The lower zone The lower zone contains the loops or 'descenders' of

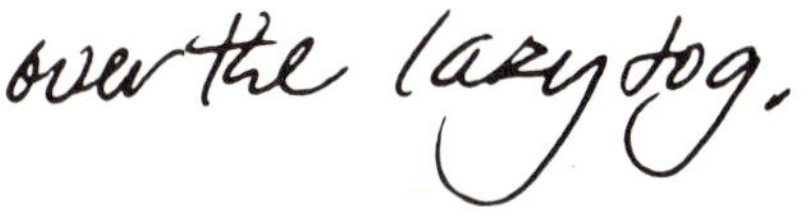

Pronounced loops in the lower zone

the 'g', 'y', 'q' and, in some cases 'z'. Since all lines which enter the lower zone are drawn towards the writer's body, it appears that all matters which have any connection with the writer's material wellbeing are expressed in this zone. Attitudes towards food, sex, conventions and traditions, money and possessions are all indicated here.
The upper zone The upper zone contains the top of all capitals and the loops or 'ascenders' of 'f', 'l', 'h', etc. Here the writer's attitude towards

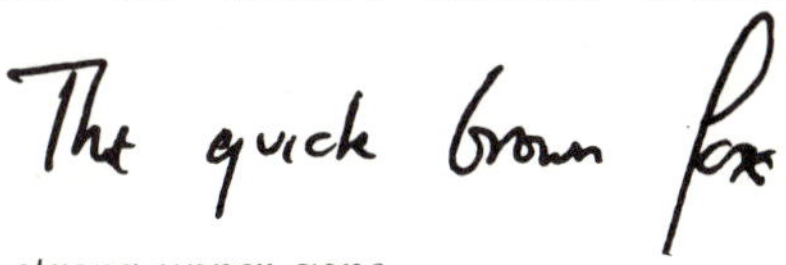

A strong upper zone

higher matters like ideals, moral values, or religion, are expressed.
The middle zone The middle zone contains all small letters. It is the most important of the three zones since some part of every letter must go through it, no matter which zone it develops into ultimately. The middle zone stands in between the entirely materialistic and the absolutely idealistic spheres. It is

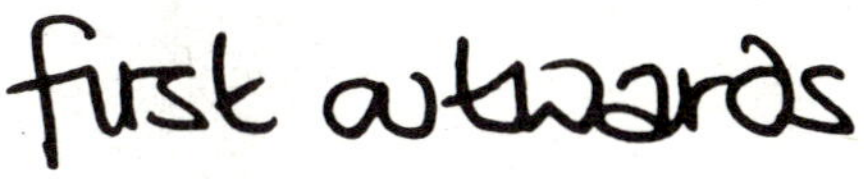

Emphasis on the middle zone

particularly significant in that it expresses the writer's attitude towards everyday matters—friends, family, work and immediate environment.
When one zone is over-emphasized, the whole balance is, of course, upset. Where there is too much on one side, there must be too little on the other. A warning is necessary here: it is dangerous to jump to conclusions. If, for example, a writing shows a greatly emphasized upper zone, do not think that the writer is necessarily an idealist. This assessment could be entirely wrong: it may only indicate great ambition. Always try to fit the meaning of each part into an all-round analysis. It is not an over-simplification to say that greatness cannot be indicated by imbalance—unless, of course, we consider ruthless dictators or successful crooks as great.
The three zones represent the writer's attitudes towards life and indicate the degree to which the writing style and movement have become habitual—in other words, unconscious or subconscious actions. It is not easy to define a subconscious action—there is a constant intermingling with conscious action. If you try to analyze your everyday activities, you will find that there are lots of things which you do without really thinking about them. This applies particularly to the way you write, unless, or course, you use 'copperplate' or 'italic' script.

MONTRÉAL, QUÉ. CANADA
AIR
PAR

The angle of lines

The zones deal with the vertical movement in writing. The next point to investigate is the left-to-right movement. Writing moves from the left towards the right hand side of the paper, as if symbolizing the 'reaching out' of the writer towards the receiver, or the 'I' towards the 'You'. Movement towards the left represents the writer's attitudes towards the past. Movement towards the right indicates attitudes towards the future. The centre is symbolic of the present, the very moment at which the pen performs the act of writing.

Delving still deeper, the left represents a subconscious attitude towards the mother-figure, since birth is, of course, the first thing in anyone's past. The left also denotes the female element within the writer's surroundings. The right expresses the attitude towards the male element, or the father. This may account for the tendency among young people suddenly to develop writing which slants towards the left during puberty. The psychological diagnosis could be that they begin to feel the growth of sexual forces which may frighten them. Consequently they shrink away from an unknown future (the right) and take refuge in the past (the left), perhaps even subconsciously wish-wishing that they were back on their mother's protective lap.

Lines

As you proceed from the left hand side of the paper to the right you produce lines of writing. The most direct way from point A to point B is the straight line. But unless you use ruled paper, you will probably waver a little, or your lines may go up, down, curve or go in steps.

Straight lines on unlined paper are a sign of steadfastness and purposefulness. In addition, this characteristic can confirm the trait of aloofness.

Wavy lines, particularly on lined paper, suggest degrees of unsteadiness, excitability, or lack of inner stability.

Curved lines indicate that the writer was tired, but pulled himself together to reach the end.

Arched lines may indicate depression or mental or physical fatigue.

Stepped lines occur very seldom; they are produced by hesitating after every syllable, or word. If the steps go up, the writer probably has doubts about the success of the purpose in mind but has sufficient pluck to try again. If the steps descend, the writer is a pessimist, expecting no positive response from anything he does.

Ascending straight lines, or even wavy ones, show energy, optimism, and self-assertion.

Descending straight lines probably show temporary depression or fatigue.

Straight lines

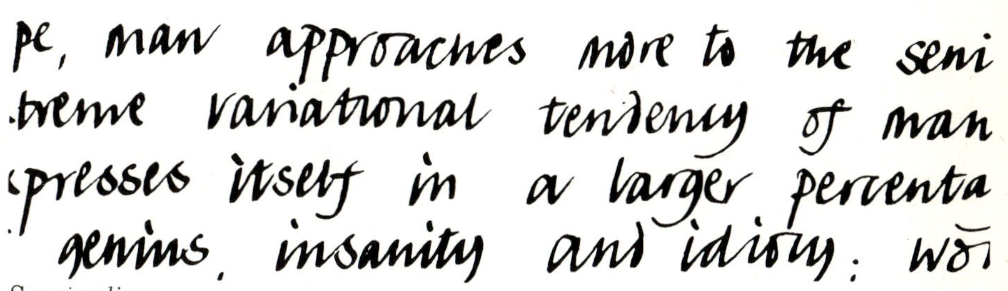

Sagging lines

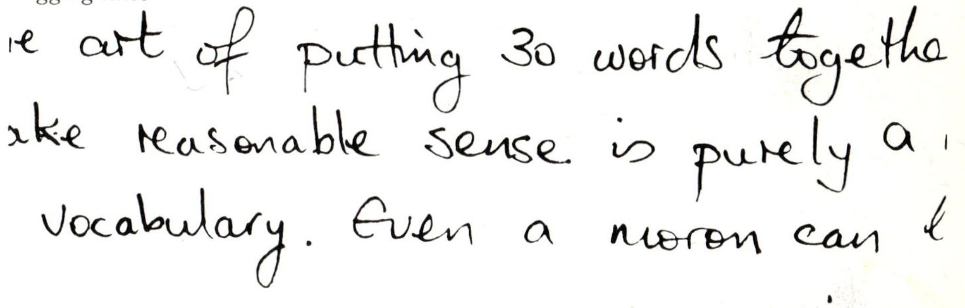

Arched lines

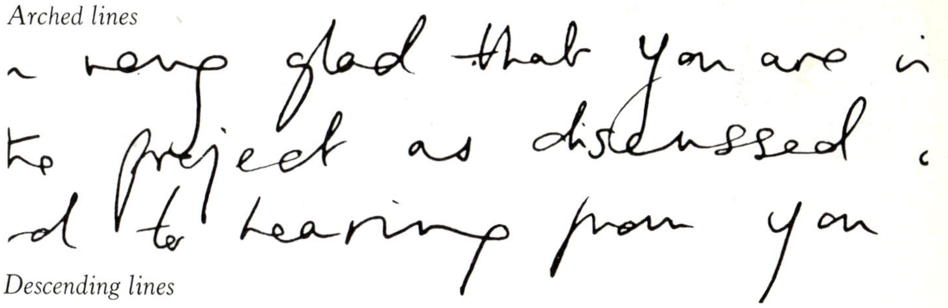

Descending lines

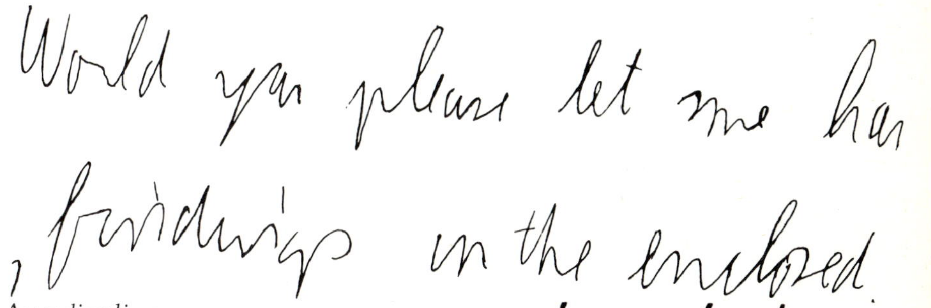

Ascending lines

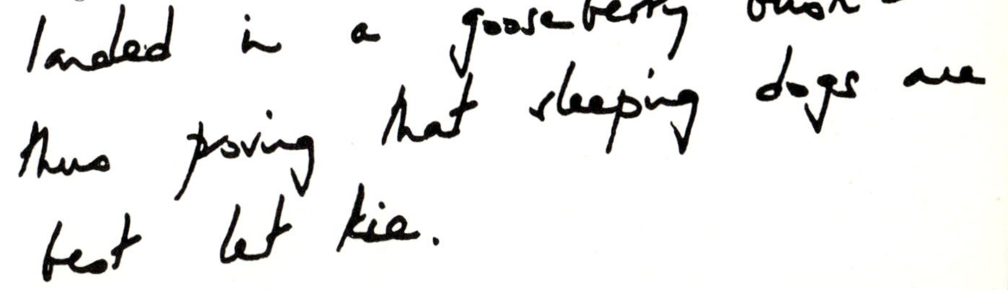

Margins

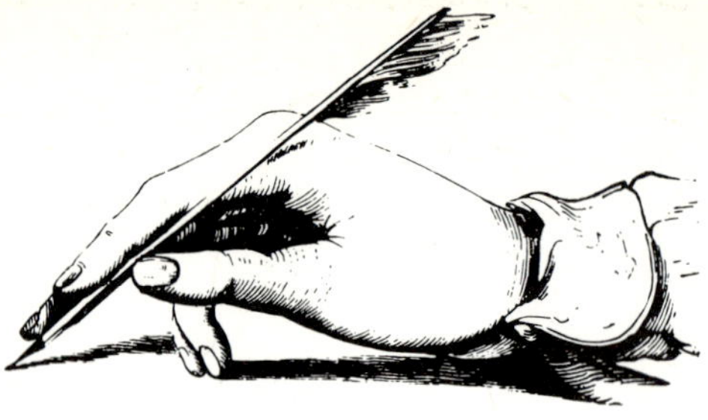

Margins follow logically from the investigation of the left-to-right movement. They are dictated by the spatial impulse and are particularly important as part of the general positive or negative impression of a page of writing. A careful, methodical writer always tries to produce a straight margin, neither too near nor too far from the paper's edge.

What margins can mean

Wide margins If the margins are wide the writer is rather extravagant, or perhaps a snob who wishes to make a good impression on the recipient.
Narrow margins If both the left and the right hand margins are narrow, the writer is economical and wants to use the page to the fullest, probably squeezing in his signature at the very bottom of the page.
Decreasing margins If a margin is reasonably wide at first and decreases as the writer fills the page — quite a common feature — it means the writer gradually withdraws from his original wish to make contact with the recipient. This may arise from modesty or a feeling of inadequacy and inferiority; or it could be because he has had unpleasant emotional experiences in the past.
Increasing margins When both margins increase towards the bottom of the page, the writer begins with generous intentions but wishes to remain distant enough to be free from influences. However, his emotions can get the better of him in spite of himself.
Irregular margins Irregular margins, particularly on the left, are relatively rare. They indicate a person who neither plans nor organizes his life carefully, is always muddled, often talks too much. This is particularly true when one line droops down at the end and interferes with the line below so that it becomes illegible.
Slanting margins Lefthand margins slanting to the right show an extrovert and optimistic personality, while the opposite indicates retreat, and a fear of the future.
Wavy or irregular margins A jerky, irregular margin indicates a restless, talkative person who is probably a bad organizer with an untidy mind. If the margins are wavy rather than jerky they show absent mindedness.

Letter slants

The next step is to assess the meaning of the angle of writing. You need to know the nationality of the writer before assessing the meaning of the angle. Most writing is taught with a slight forward slant, though British school children generally learn an upright script. Use a protractor to measure the degree of slant and find the average throughout the writing, since it is inclined to vary.
If the writing is very upright it can be considered as a slight leftward movement if the school model slants rightwards. If an upright school model is adhered to it indicates self-control and reticence.

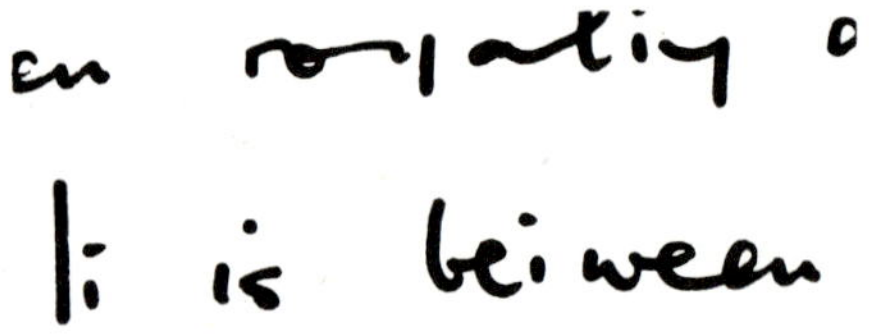

Upright writing

The forward slope

It seems natural that a writer who wishes to convey something to someone should instinctively lean towards the right, as if trying to get close to the

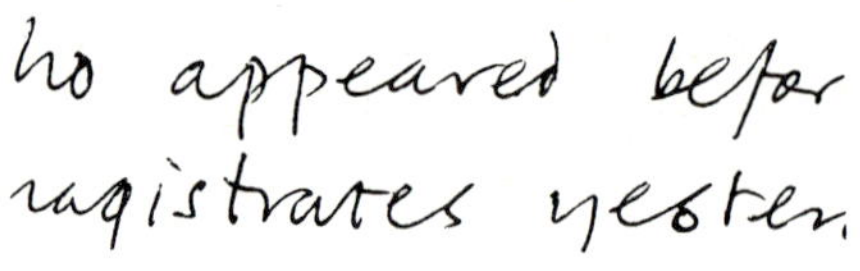

A positive forward slope

person to whom he is writing. This feeling for contact is particularly strong when a British person's writing slopes to the right. But if the slope is exaggerated, and the writing almost falls on to the line, an obsessive nature is indicated.

The backward slope

When the slope is backward, the writer is shy and afraid to show his real feelings, but he may also be hesitant to face the consequences of his statements.

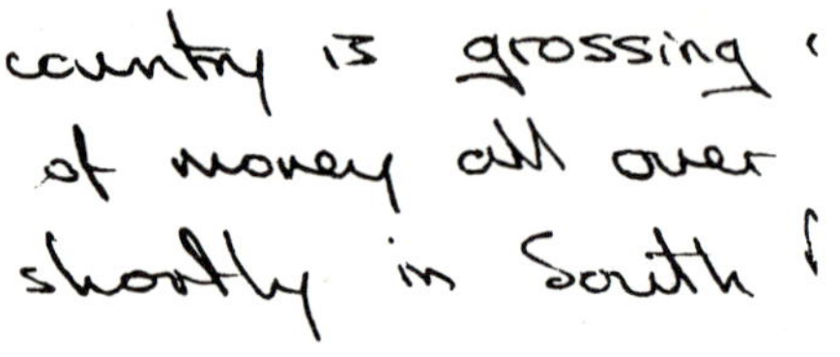

Left-sloping writing

The Left-or-right significance

You should also apply the findings which relate to left and right, remembering that the left is the female element or past, the right the male or

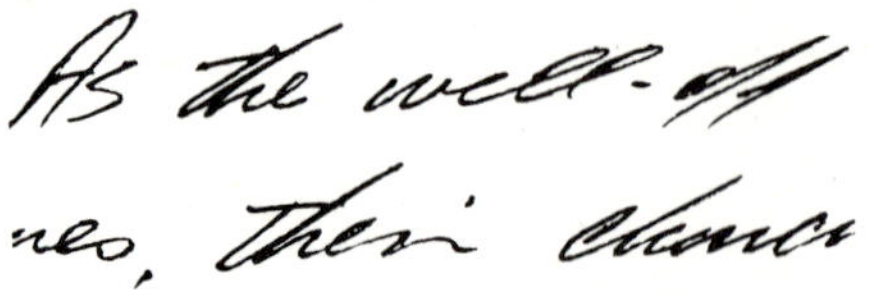

Extreme rightward slope

future—the negative and positive poles. In backward sloping writing this could show an unwillingness to face the reality of the present; in forward sloping writing, a dominant personality is indicated—ambitious, forward-looking but possibly also domineering.

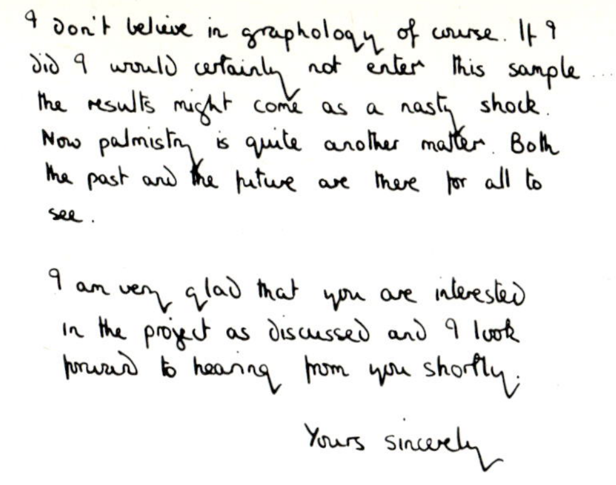

Increasing margins

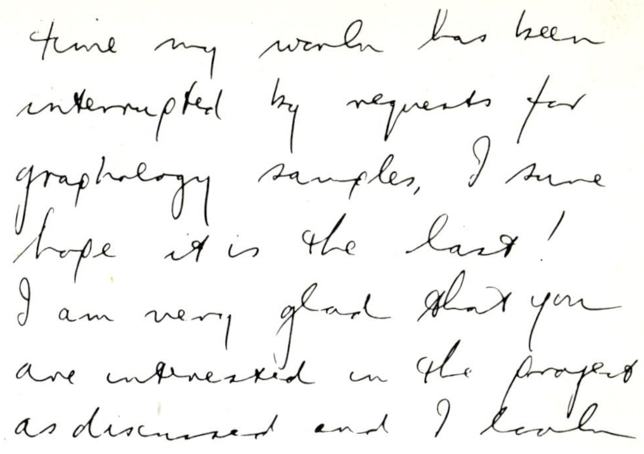

Very narrow margins

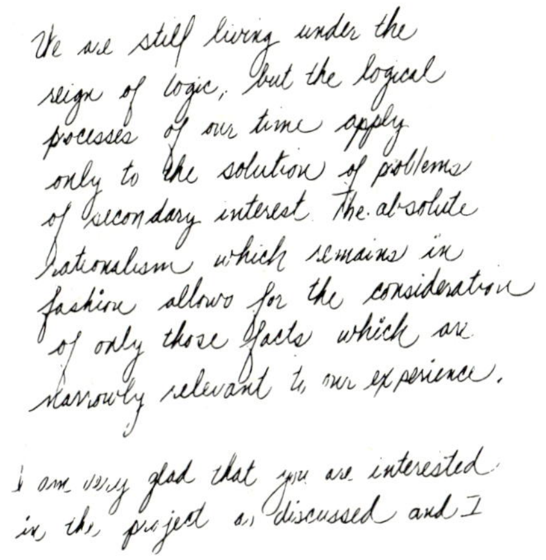

Irregular, wide margin

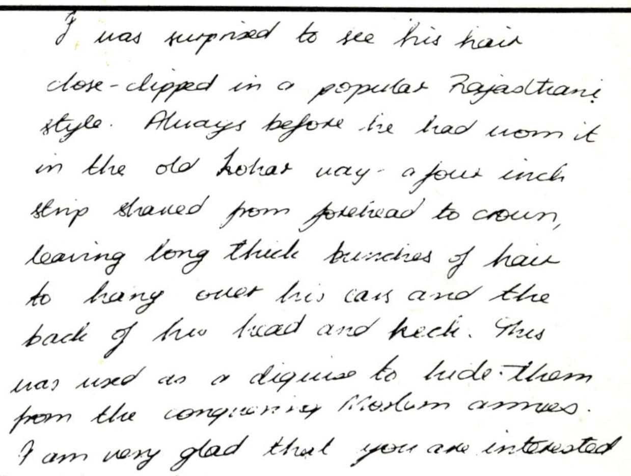

Decreasing margins

Addressing envelopes

The purpose of the address on an envelope is of course to ensure that a letter reaches its destination without difficulty. It is natural therefore to write envelopes more clearly and distinctly than the letters inside — some people even use capital letters to make quite sure. However, a surprising percentage of people address their envelopes so indistinctly that it would need an expert in codes to decipher them. The way the envelope is written is a useful confirmation of findings arrived at through analysis of other writing.

The position of the address

To interpret envelopes graphologically, the same techniques apply as for general writing analysis — the zonal arrangements, and the left-right aspects, together with the assessment of the whole writing. A reasonable, well-balanced person arranges his envelope neatly, placing the name and address in the centre, or slightly to the left, leaving ample margins all round.

Some people write the address at the top of the envelope, too close to the postage stamp, making the envelope practically useless. These people are constantly losing the ground under foot and lack a firm grasp of reality.

The writer who places the address near the bottom of the envelope is too dependent upon the material world, and will be easily depressed by business or financial affairs which he has difficulty in managing well.

Some writers place the address too far left. The left is symbolic of the past, the 'mother' attachment, and it is not surprising that these writers are not confident about the future. They shy away from the right, from contact with society. They prefer to arrange matters in their own way, not asking for help. They are unforthcoming and not particularly friendly. The past has more meaning for them than the future, and they treat the present suspiciously.

When the address is placed too far right, the writer is anxious to make contact with society. He is an extrovert, anxious and eager to find someone he can rely on to assist him in managing life. He may indeed rely more on others than on himself, hoping others will pick his chestnuts out of the fire for him.

The size of writing

Most people make an extra effort to write clearly on envelopes, even printing the address in capitals, to be sure the letter arrives safely. However, if the writing on the envelope is smaller than that used in the actual letter, the writer loses self-confidence when confronted with strangers and unfamiliar situations, particularly in his social life. On the other hand, he may prefer to keep his real feelings to himself. When the address is larger, the writer may be overbearing, vain and excitable, keeping up an insincere pose of self-assurance.

How letters are joined

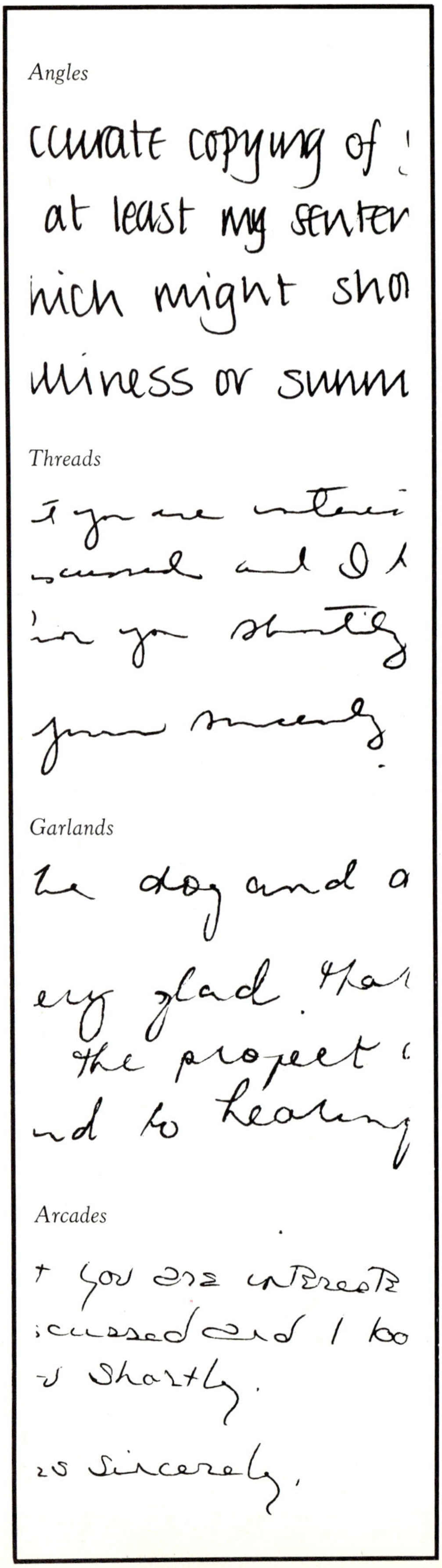

Most textbooks of graphology agree that one of the most important features in handwriting analysis is the form of connection that links the individual letters into words. These connections usually occur in the middle zone and are made with curves or angles.

Once again, a knowledge of nationality is essential. For example, the German school model until the late nineteen-thirties was angular. Therefore a German national born in the first half of the twentieth century would still use this form of connection, even when writing in a foreign language. Italic script demands angular connections as well, whereas the sort of copperplate script taught in most North American schools relies on garlands. Connections are revealing because they occur in the middle zone. The way they are shaped, the forms they assume, are most revealing. From them you can analyze the writer's degree of adaptation to his environment, his partners, his profession and life in general.

Types of connection

The garland This is the most frequent, allowing the down-stroke to connect the following up-stroke in a flowing, rhythmical movement from left to right. The garland suggests the receptiveness of a bowl; its curve towards the upper zone suggests that the writer is open to the influence of ideals. It is also a fluent left-to-right movement, and a pure garland writing shows openness to spiritual, emotional and social influences. Garlands vary a great deal and should be interpreted accordingly; they can be firm or loose, looped or sharp, narrow or wide.

Garland writers have a natural relationship with the world around them and are open to influences from outside. Impressionable and adaptable, they try to avoid unnecessary conflict.

The arcade This is the opposite of the garland. Its curves are closed towards the upper zone and open towards the lower zone. The arcade writer tries to close himself off from the outside world. He has his own way of adapting himself to the world around him, but never discloses his inner self. The writer of arcades places more importance on form and behaviour — aesthetic as well as social — than on the contents of his letter. Members of the aristocracy, royalty and high clergy often use arcades. Many criminals use them because they have reasons for not disclosing their private lives. Artists, particularly craftsmen and designers, are often arcade writers.

It is difficult to establish emotional contact with someone whose writing contains arcades, no matter which of the many variations of them he uses. Such people often feel embarrassed by personal questions and will answer with reticence or overdone politeness, giving the impression that the questioner is prying.

Angled connections These differ from garlands and arcades, both of which are curved movements that flow naturally from the pen. The angular connection impedes the even flow, because the hand has to stop for a moment to turn the nib and make the angular spike. Garlands and arcades represent forms of adaptation, while angles express a refusal to adapt, an element of opposition or an inability to react to stimuli as expected. Angular writers have little sense of obligation to the world; they oppose it by their very angularity. But these writers make no attempt to shirk obstacles — they often look for hindrances for the fun of overcoming them and they prefer difficulty to smoothness. People of great will-power use this form of connection, requiring the world to adapt to them.

The threaded connection This is neither angular or flowing, and if the whole script shows nothing but threads, it becomes illegible. Threads increase the speed of the writing, and are used by people for whom time is precious. If threads occur at the end of words instead of the last syllable or final letters, the writer expects the reader to be intelligent enough to grasp the meaning of a word by its context and may be paying him a compliment. However, a writer who uses threads can also be an opportunist with few convictions, someone who wants to better himself at any cost.

Connection and disconnection

A writer who sits down to send a letter lets his pen flow from left to right without thinking of anything but the

message he wishes to convey. The act of writing is quite automatic. If his thoughts flow freely, his writing will also and he will produce a well-connected script. If he is a cautious, pedantic person, a perfectionist or someone who is afraid that his image may suffer if he puts down his thoughts freely, some of the letters will be disconnected.

Within the same writing some words are fully connected and others seem to consist of disconnected syllables or letters. Establish to what degree the writing is connected, remembering that some people have a 'word-impulse' and others a 'syllable-impulse'. This means that the motor impulse moves the pen through whole words, or through one syllable at a time. In addition, ascertain the width of the distances between words. These gaps are as important as the spaces between lines.

Partially-connected writing If a writing shows a good flow, but the letters are only partially connected, the writer thinks before he acts; he takes a deep breath between thoughts. A writer with a 'syllable-impulse' is an intelligent person who pauses to think and wishes to make himself clear by choosing the right words. This may indicate thoroughness, or he may be a calculating person who plans his impression on others with care.

Disconnected writing If a writing is completely disconnected you have a shy, idealistic person who does not find it easy to have free relationships, especially intimate ones. You rarely find a disconnected script with a large lower zonal development: this is quite logical, since the lower zone indicates the degree of material pleasure hoped for. Disconnected writers often have very wide spaces between their lines: they actually try to avoid any social contact at all and place a vacuum around themselves. Disconnection slows the writing flow as well.

Connected writing A social person who likes to talk and meet others will have well-connected writing, with some breathing spaces which do not affect its legibility.

Space between words Wide spaces between words in which letters are only partly connected indicate reserve, shyness and perhaps caution, as well as thoughtfulness. Narrow spaces may show lack of reserve, impatience, self-confidence and action. If the words are actually joined by an extra stroke, so that the pen never actually leaves the paper, it shows a talkative person, who could be a busybody. It certainly shows someone who has much to communicate.

Fully connected writing

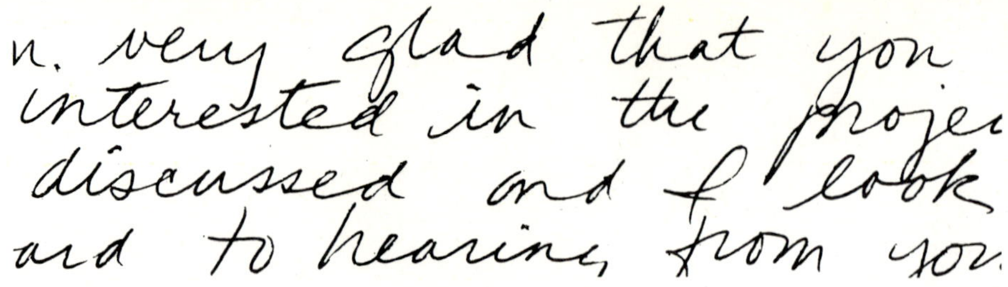

Partially connected writing

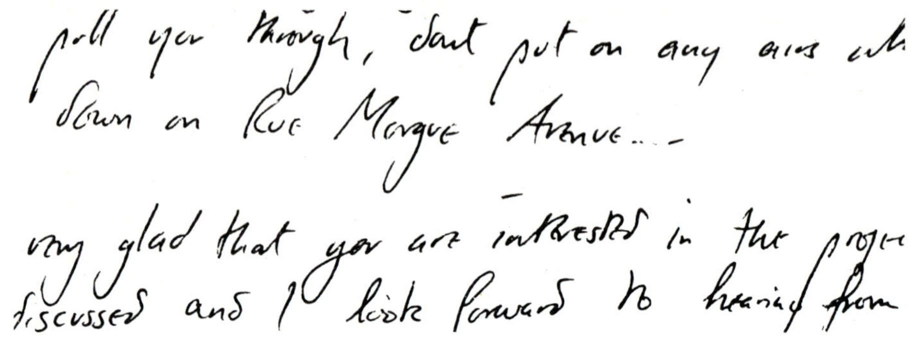

Disconnected writing

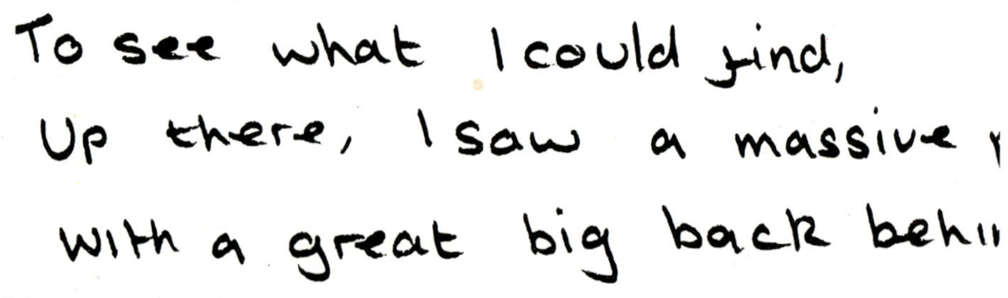

Narrow word spacing

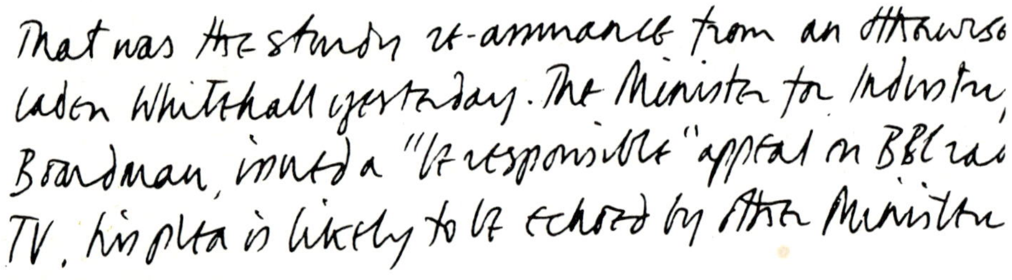

Connected words

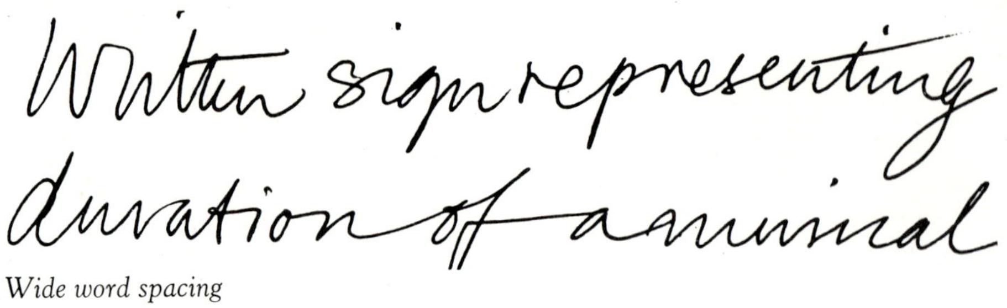

Wide word spacing

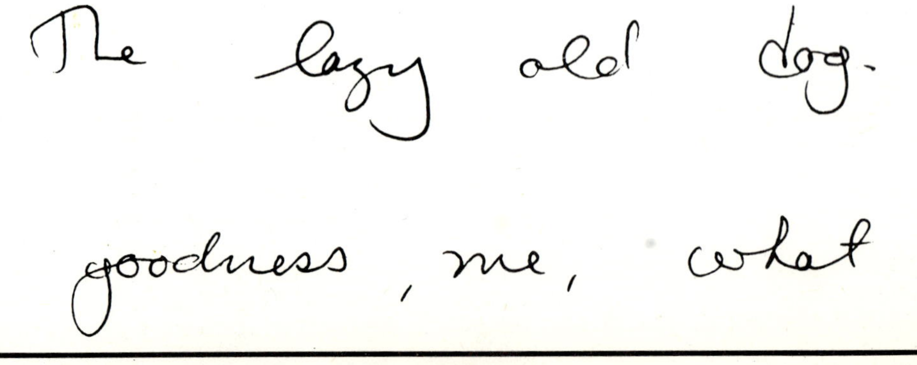

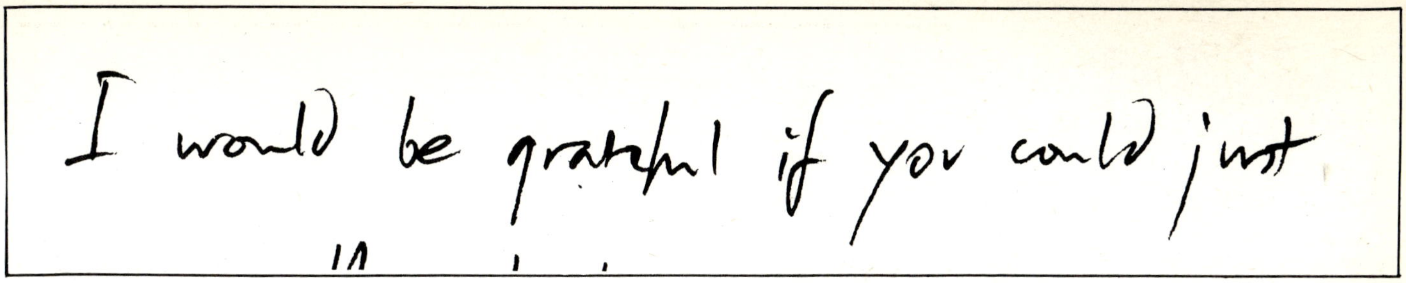

Anthony Last
Age: 26
Occupation: Printer

Specific features:
Small, but speedy writing.
Letter formations intelligently simplified.
Sharp angles, mixed with arcades and garlands.
Small left-hand margin.

Analysis:
This is a highly strung man with ambitions. He is a fine organizer and visual planner. This means he possesses a visual imagination which he tries to put into practice, constantly fighting against his enemy, time. He is the type who is fun to work with – but not so funny to work under, because he expects others to be as quick on the uptake as he is himself. He does not suffer fools gladly. (He himself hates to work under anybody).
He can be rather obstreperous when interfered with because he is sensitive and intuitive and hates it when someone interferes with his free-flowing imagination. At the same time one will find him to be a realist and a very practical person – one who works best when under stress or pressure. Very honest and sincere, he is also discreet and capable of keeping a secret – as good a friend as he can be a fierce enemy.

Désirée Swain
Age: 21
Occupation: Secretary

Specific features:
Lower Zone neglected. Hesitant connections.
Bent 'f' formations. Indistinct forms of connection.

Analysis:
The writer is a shy, but very sincere person who as yet has not found the strength of self conviction necessary to fulfil all her aspirations. She is basically a sincere idealist, but because she has not yet the courage of her own convictions she is usually a little on the defensive. And her defensive remarks are at times a little too blunt and outspoken. One will find that she is somewhat jealous of people who seem to be more adequate to cope with the complexities of life. This will change as she gains experience and confidence. She is conscientious, prepared to work hard, and eager to please her superiors – even if she somehow hates them for being superiors. She may be a little moody but she is at heart decent, a little naive and a very nice, honest young lady.

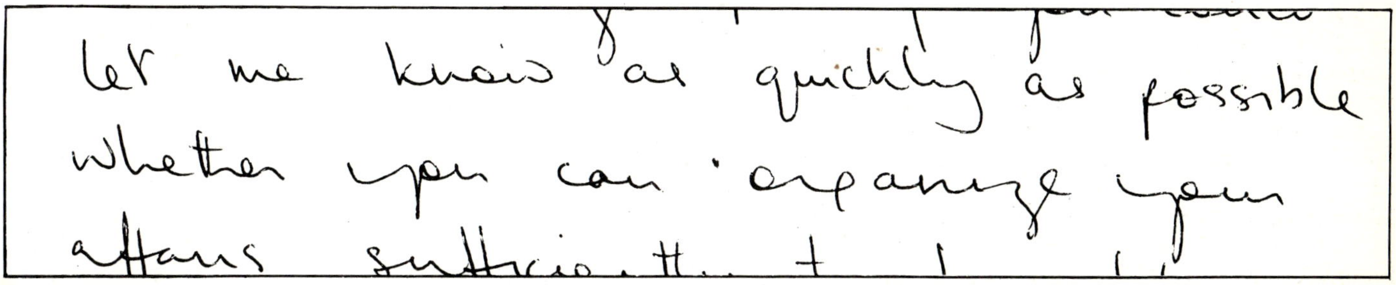

Elizabeth Walker
Age: 28
Occupation: Managing Editor

Specific features:
Threaded forms of connection.
Right-hand margin irregular.
Lower zone emphasized.
Some disconnections.
Fast.

Analysis:
The writer is a delightful, highly intelligent, scatterbrain who is capable of talking the hindlegs off a donkey. Her mind is a quick and perceptive one. It is not easy to fool her, but one is much more likely to be fooled by her, or at least roped in to assist her in completing one of her schemes which she has no time to complete herself. She always seems to have a variety of plans in hand, and a combination of her drive and her charm enable her to complete most of them with the help of others. Free and easy going as she may be, she knows very well what she wants, and when it comes to assessing the monetary rewards due to her, one will find that she knows very well what she is worth. In other words she has excellent common sense and her attitudes to work and people around her are the result of experience and, perhaps, clever scheming.
She may be vague, but never dishonest. If she occasionally seems a little forgetful this is not intentional, but the result of having just a little too much on her plate.

Width

The width or extension of the writing is expressed in the middle zone, and from it one analyzes the writer's generosity, emotional equilibrium and, if the pressure of the pen is firm, energy and willpower.

Wide writing

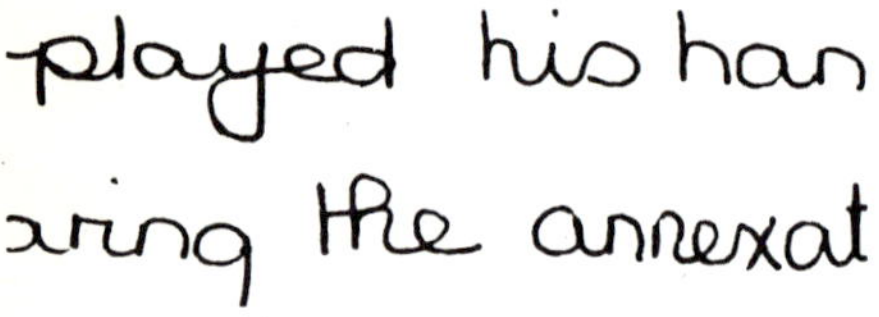

If the writing is wide, but the letter-formations are neglected, its rhythm weak, and large margins are thrown in for good measure, the writer is wasteful and extravagant. If width is combined with genuine garland connections, generosity and self-sacrifice are indicated. When the ending of the last stroke of a word or line is elongated, sociability and determination are shown. On the other hand, if individual letters are unduly wide and large, arrogance and pretension are indicated. But when the writing is fluent, the connections easy, and the i-dots or t-strokes part of the connection, it means versatility.

Narrow writing

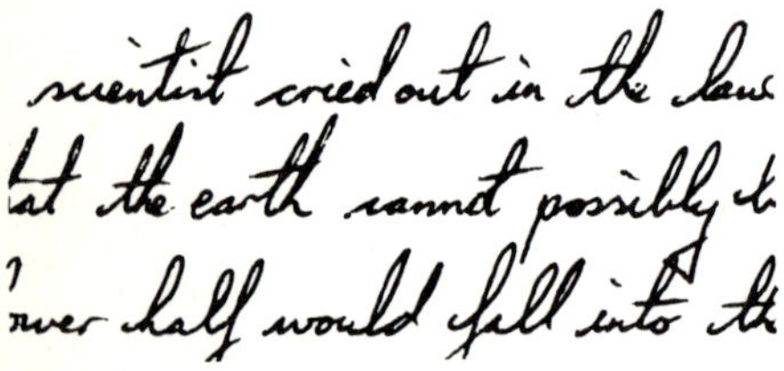

Narrowness is also expressed in the middle zone. When fast, rhythmic writing with angular connections is narrow, the writer is determined and self-controlled.

If narrowness occurs in an upright script with low placed i-dots slightly ahead of the stem, the writer will be distrustful. A tight slow writing with a leftward slant or movement, shows narrow-mindedness and probably self-fishness. The writer may also bear grudges. When many end-strokes are missing and the whole script looks disjointed, avarice and miserliness can be expected. Narrowness combined with weak pressure indicate shyness.

Speed

The speed of writing can be deduced from a combination of many of the individual writing characteristics already discussed. Of course, most quick writing shows signs of hesitation and even the slowest writers have a certain rhythm to keep their writing at a steady pace. However, there are general points which can differentiate between fast and slow writing.

Quick writing

Quick writing usually shows many of the following characteristics. Smooth, unbroken strokes and rounded forms connected by garlands, arcades or — more especially — threads, show speed and a good flowing rhythm. Frequent signs of rightward movement obviously indicate speed, since the writer is anxious to get to the end of one line and carry his ideas on to the next. This can also be combined with a slight leftward movement at the end of a line when the end of the sentence is on the next line. Letters which are joined by t-bars, and words joined by light strokes (showing that the pen has not even left the paper) are also signs of speed. Any simplification of letter forms speeds up the writing process — and this often manifests itself as a complete curtailing of letters at the ends of words, almost to the point of illegibility. Other characteristics of quick writing are widening of the left hand margin; no initial or final embellishments; rising lines — even though the writing remains at a constant angle — and wide distances between letters, especially if the script itself is narrow. It is unusual to find writing which shows all these points; in fact, it would indicate a hasty, agitated person who is nervous almost to the point of being unbalanced. But if the writing is legible as well as quick it shows that the writer has some control over his natural exuberance, is generally well-balanced and socially adjusted.

Slow writing

Anything which stops the natural movement of the pen across the pages could be considered a sign of slow writing, though the way in which letters are formed in our alphabet often necessitates certain stops, hesitations and leftward movements. For instance, i-dots and t-bars have to be indicated even if only in the most rudimentary way, since illegibility and confusion can occur if they are absent. If i-dots and t-bars are habitually missing, the writer is either thoughtless or scatter-brained. Other signs in the handwriting will establish which is the case. However, very carefully placed i-dots and t-bars are two of the many things which can slow writing down. Wavering forms and broken strokes indicate slow writing and suggest inhibition and lack of co-ordination. Frequent leftward movements and frequent pauses indicated by meaningless blobs, angles, and divided or touched-up letters are further indications of slow handwriting. Embellishments and enrichments of all kinds obviously slow the writing though creative embellishments often do not actually impair the rhythm. Signs of slowness are indicated by sinking lines, light pressure and pasty writing. If some of these signs are incorporated into an otherwise quick hand, the writer is moody and changeable, restless or impatient. Slow writing without embellishment indicates a person who is slow-thinking but thorough — not wanting to be hurried and using logic rather than impulse to make decisions. He has an even temperament and is reliable.

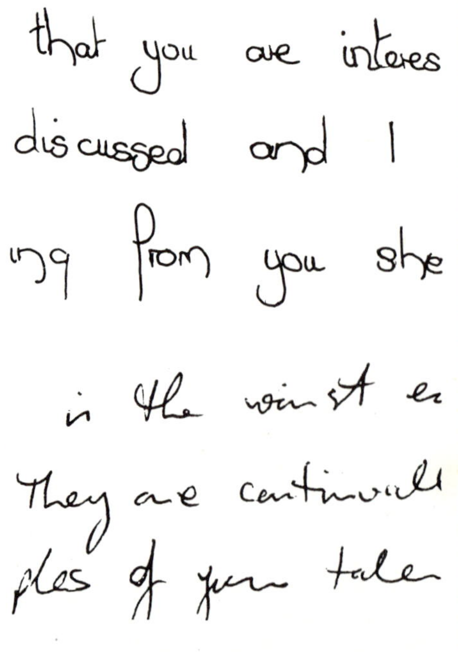

Above: Two examples of fast and slow writing. Top: a typical slow script, carefully formed, very legible, but with some enriched letters — note the 'n' and 'h' formations. Bottom: fast writing with threaded connections and strong rightward trends.

Letter sizes

To examine the size and width of writing, you need a ruler, a compass and a good magnifying glass, without which some finer points may escape you. It is not only the size which is important, but also the relative sizes of the zones. Most school models show the relationship between the middle zone and the upper and lower zones as about 1:3; that is, middle zone letters should be roughly one third the size of the ascenders and descenders. In England, the ratio is usually 1:2.

Sometimes a writer shows a large middle zone with a small lower or upper zone. This can give the impression of a generally small writing. In this case, return to the interpretation of the three zones, and work out how they apply specifically to that writer. Generally speaking, considerable difference in zonal size shows an element of unrest.

There are also two kinds of large writing: relative and absolute. Relative largeness occurs when the middle zone is disproportionately large, absolute largeness refers to writing which is big in all three zones.

In a normal-sized writing, the relationship between the zones is harmonious and spacing is good; margins and lines are well-formed and straight, and the impression is that the writer is realistic and positive. The writing appears neither large nor small.

Large or small?

It is not surprising that the size of the writing indicates the writer's sense of self-importance. Often a writer makes up for the lack of acknowledgement from society by producing large writing. If the lower zone letters are badly formed or neglected, and loops are absent in the upper zone, this means that the writer is unhappy, and that his aims and ambitions have remained unfulfilled. Whether this is mainly his fault or due to other circumstances can often be established by other factors in the writing.

'Absolute' small writing

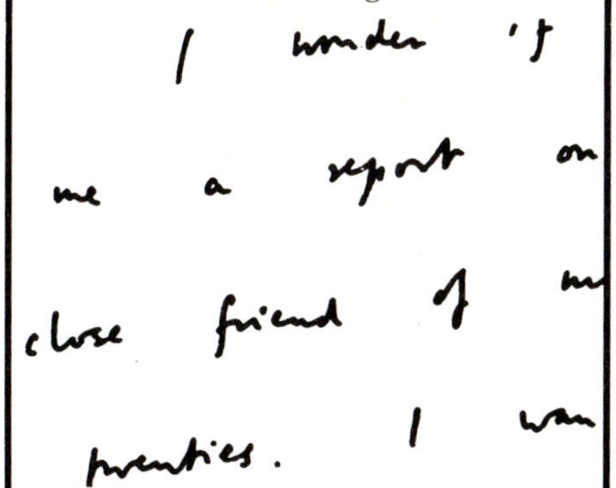

Small middle zone writing

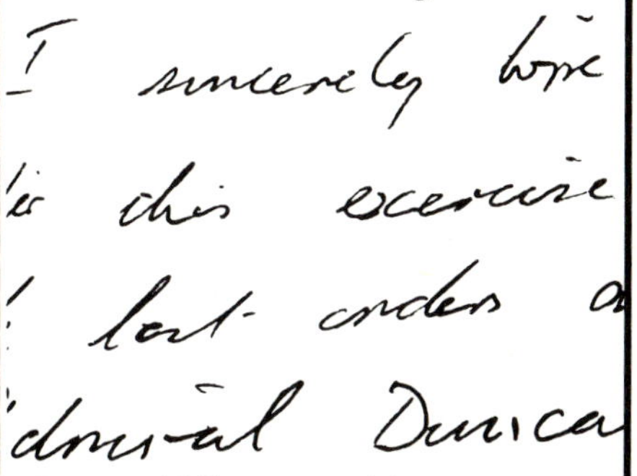

Large middle zone writing

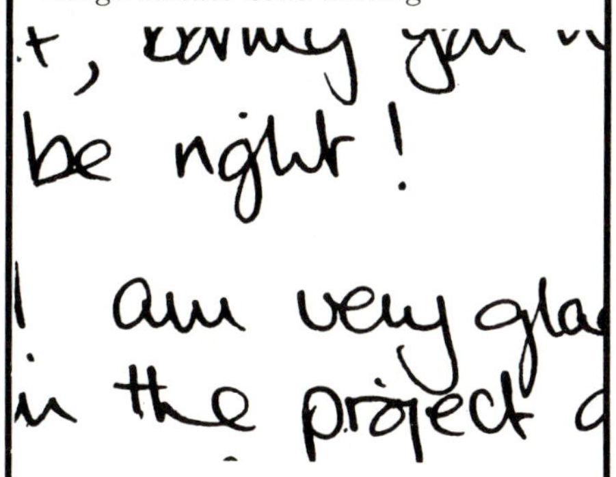

'Absolute' large writing

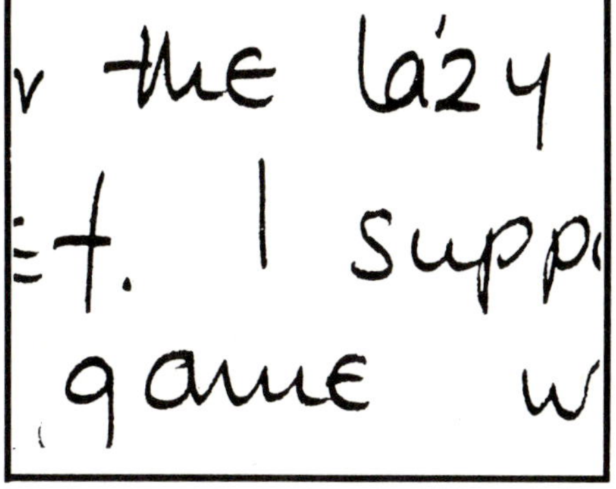

A small, well-shaped middle zone which is well-organized in its space, indicates an intelligent, critical person, with some specialized knowledge. He is modest, but knows what he wants and is prepared to work for it. On the other hand, small writing may indicate a modest, introverted character, who does not stand out in a crowd. Or, when other indications confirm it, a writer who suffers from fears, shows a lack of self-respect and has a subordinate attitude towards society.

Space between lines

A well-organized page of writing is obviously the work of a well-organized mind. The lines should be sufficiently spaced to give the page an orderly and pleasing appearance. The descenders of one line should not interfere with the ascenders of the line below it.

If the lines are too close the zones become interwoven and illegibility follows. This often happens when people use a large, extravagant hand — people who write like this often talk too much and are uneconomical in many ways.

If the lines are very far apart, they indicate isolation, detachment and a degree of reserve which could become anti-social. This could be caused by shyness, bad conscience or mental disorientation, but whatever the case may be, it spells difficulty in coming to grips with reality. It also implies some extravagance or mismanagement of affairs.

Very close lines are illegible.

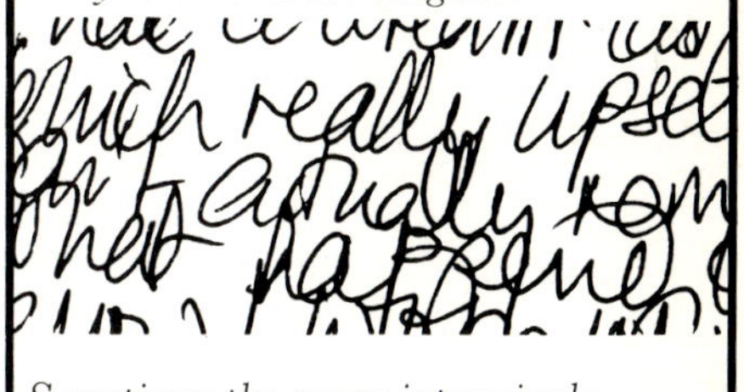

Sometimes the zones intermingle.

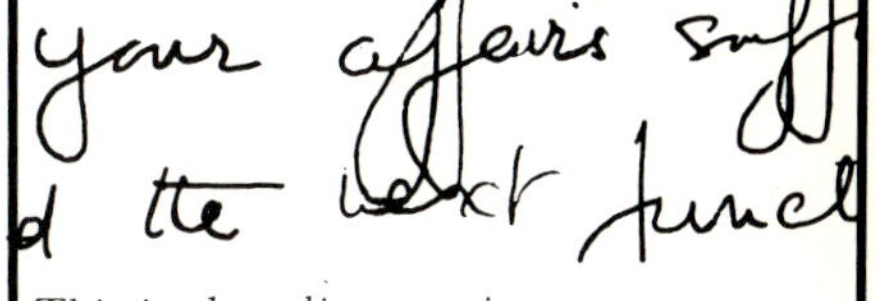

This is clear line spacing.

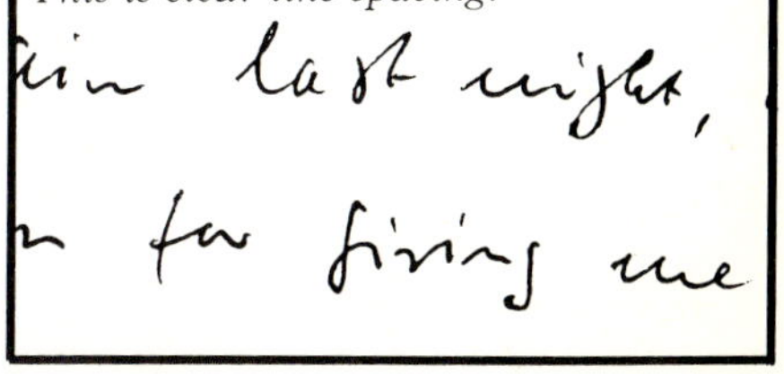

The colour of the ink

Most people use blue-black ink to write a letter, but now and then a letter arrives in the post written in red, blue, green or brown ink. No doubt an odd colour ink gives writing a special face, and the colour chosen gives another clue to the kind of person who is writing.

Light blue ink indicates that the writer has spiritual rather than material interests. He may be religious and have a deep understanding of people's problems.

Blue-black ink is preferred by rational, conservative people, who are probably in business and adher to conventions and traditions. They do not want to be different from others, so they use the universal colour.

Black ink contrasts strongly with most notepapers, especially white, and writers who use it are making sure that their statements are noted.

Red is symbolic of strength, vitality and energy. It also represents affection; hence red roses to a lady-love. Certainly a person who uses red ink wants to be different, to stand out. In a bold script this may indicate some pomposity, but if a business executive uses red ink, he likes action and has an original approach.

Green is connected with harmony, adaptability and versatility. People with extra-sensory powers often choose green as their favourite shade. Young people frequently have a phase when they write in green ink, sometimes indicating an inferiority complex. Usually it is women who use green ink, or slightly effeminate men. One needs to try to understand why such a writer needs to stand out from the crowd.

Brown ink is rare, but the writer who uses it is often a man who has 'arrived'. He is likely to be an aristocrat or at the top of his profession. Brown ink leaves the impression of authority; but beware. Shrewd, professional men know how to impress, and a letter from a businessman in brown ink may be a bluff.

PETER ANDERSON

Pressure

Pressure is another important aspect of handwriting analysis since it shows much about the writer's will and vitality — in psychological terms his 'libido'. If pressure is very heavy, it indicates strength or will. It shows irritability or alternatively a slow, heavy-going personality. Sudden, dagger-like pressure formations indicate a tendency towards violence. Random and unnecessary heavy pressure which disturbs the harmony of the writing as a whole indicates maliciousness, or at least pretentiousness.

It is sometimes hard to distinguish the degree of pressure. When a pen is correctly held, there is a difference in shading between the up-strokes and the down-strokes, because the pressure is naturally stronger in the down-strokes. It is a good idea to find out how

Thick and pasty: this shows sensuality
Fine and sharp: a very sensitive writer

the various characteristics have been formed. Follow the movement and flow of the writing with an orange stick or toothpick. This is especially useful when assessing writing in felt-tip — you will be able to feel the emphasis depending on the relative weights of the ascenders and descenders.

'Pasty' writing — in which both the up-stroke and the down-stroke are equal in weight, looks somewhat smeary and lacks shading. It is a sign of heavy, even pressure. Look carefully at the originality of the deviations from the school model. Such writers may be greedy, perverted in some way, or uninhibited.

'Sharp' script which is fine and spidery, an indication of light pressure, shows a hypersensitive person — an inhibited writer who may have moral prejudices, a mystic or ascetic.

Pasty writing indicates sensuality, while sharpness denotes aestheticism. Of course, this doesn't mean a gourmet cannot be an aesthete, on the contrary, but both will find pleasure in quite a different way and for entirely different reasons. Aestheticism is difficult to define. A poet may find pop music anything but enjoyable, but this does not mean that pop stars do not find pleasure in reading poetry. It is a question of sensitivity rather than adherence to tradition, and adds weight to the point made already that the graphologist must not pre-judge, but analyze letter-formations as he finds them. No one is completely without prejudices, but everyone should try to be objective when the task is to understand other people. You may disagree with their outlook to life, but if you understand something of why and how they arrive at their views it helps towards a more tolerant view of life, and you may be able to help the other chap when he finds himself at loggerheads with the world.

Pens and pressure

The degree of pressure can be affected by the writing instrument. In script written with a felt-tip pen, it is very difficult to detect light and heavy strokes, though use of a magnifying glass will help to show the difference of thicks and thins. But ask yourself what sort of person might prefer to use a felt-tip pen rather than any other. The choice of pen provides immediate clues to the writer's make-up. If the writing is by ballpoint pen, turn the paper over and feel the impression with your fingertips.

Many people still prefer to write personal letters with a fountain pen. They feel that the instrument, and the ink flowing from it, give the letter a more personal note, and the feel of pen pressing into paper, producing light- and shadow-strokes, is a pleasurable experience. People who prefer to write with an ink pen are likely to be more fastidious than the down-to-earth types who write with ball-point pens, which are easier to use.

Simple or ornate

It is obvious that embellishments or enrichments will cause writing delays, because any movement which adds unnecessary curves or spirals to the formation of letters contributes to a slowing-down of the writing flow. Simplifications have the opposite effect. An intelligent person will try to reach his goal by the quickest route. Over-simplification — to the point of illegibility — may point to someone who needs to show off, trying anything to get attention. Someone who is competent and well-balanced has no need to embellish his ego.

The kind of impression that an embellished writing makes depends, of course, on the recipient, and on whether the enrichments are executed with skill and taste. Embellishments could indicate an important person who likes ceremony and fuss, a writer with a personal fantasy for which he has not found the right outlet, or someone who needs to boost his ego or social position. Sometimes a few letters in an otherwise well-shaped script are written differently within a word. A versatile and intelligent person probably uses this common form of enrichment. Capable of tackling complex problems efficiently, he is inventive and original, attacking every project with zest. This phenomenon, usually involves 'e', 'a', 'd', and 't', especially the Greek 'eta' and 'delta'.

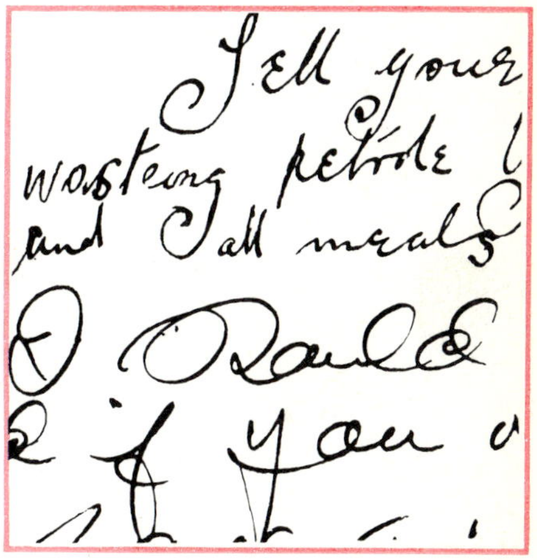

Top: These embellishments show a fussy character. Below: These show someone who needs to boost his ego.

Legibility

Writing must be legible otherwise it ceases to communicate its message. If it is written in haste or is malformed, it goes against its own purpose by being illegible. To establish the degree of legibility of a specimen of writing, you must take the words apart and see if you can decipher every syllable when they are taken out of context. If you can read every part of a word quite clearly, you have an absolutely legible writing. However, it is not enough to examine just one word — you must look at a number of multi-syllable words. Illegibility can occur in any of the three zones, and it is not good enough to examine just the middle zone, even though it is here that most evidence comes to light.

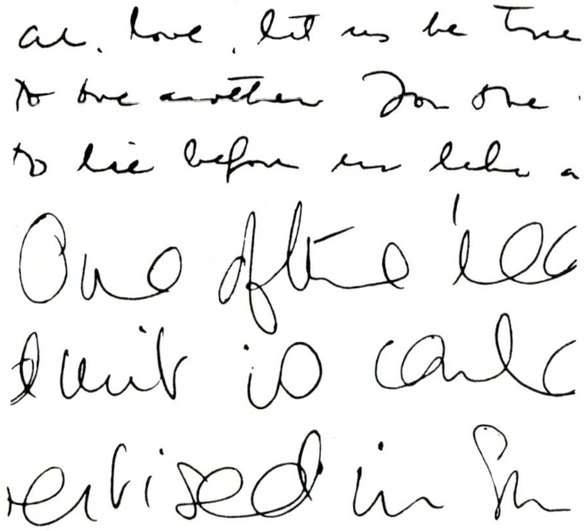

Illegibility comes in all shapes and sizes!

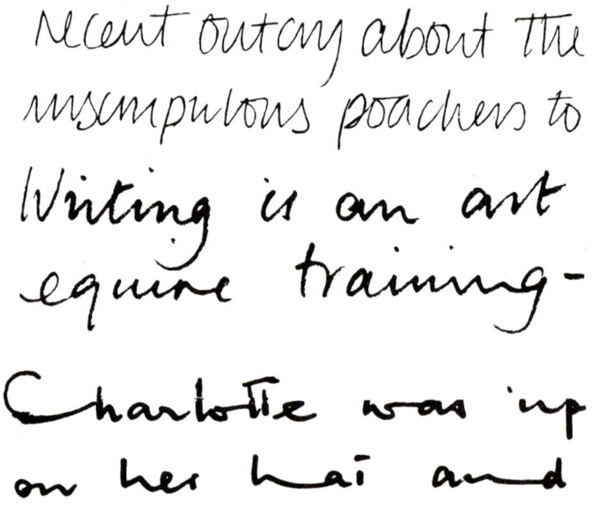

Legible writing will always communicate its message.

Legibility shows natural consideration and balance. Most people have an acceptable degree of illegibility arising from simplification of letter forms. We all expect anyone reading our writing to have sufficient common sense to understand the message through its context to some extent. Absolute legibility need not necessarily be a recommendation — the writer may simply be conventional, pedantic, fussy or slow. But it is also a sign of reliability. Double rolled 'a' and 'o' formations, combined with arcaded forms of connection in legible writing, may be signs of dishonesty. A writer may only be dishonest in his emotional reactions, due to personal disappointments and setbacks. He may be perfectly reliable in practical matters. To establish which interpretation applies, find out how the upper and lower zones were formed by following the flow of the writing with an orange-stick or toothpick.

When legible writing shows delicately-formed loops and arcaded connections of high standard, the writer is a thoughtful person, unlikely to say anything tactless or hurtful. If the middle-zone letters increase in size, and the writing has a forward slant combined with a wide first letter, we find a writer who is zealous about morality, likes to play 'first fiddle', and may put moral values before his other duties. When the first letter is very high, and the i-dots very weak, we find a shy person who suffers from self-deception. If, however, intelligent simplifications are used which do not interfere with legibility, we find a writer who sets aside personal interests for the common good.

Illegibility

There are definite degrees of illegibility in writing — from one or two words which are difficult to decipher to totally incomprehensible scribble. It is irrational to write a message which cannot be clearly understood. We must investigate what kind of person produces an illegible script and why. The illegible writer is just as anxious that his letter should arrive at its destination as the legible writer. Illegibility is caused by an unconscious action and indicates difficulty in observing ordinary social conventions. The writer shows reluctance to adapt to people and situations, and may be tactless or clumsy as well.

There are also people who, for deep and complex reasons, believe that the message they can give to the world is so involved that nobody will comprehend its esoteric meaning anyway, and so they do not bother to write clearly in the first place.

More often than not it is the speed of the writing that renders it hard to decipher. Speed creates threadlike formations — a sort of shorthand if you like — and thus an awkward deviation from the norm. A small hand with many threadlike formations indicates a hypersensitive person. However, if only the endings of words are neglected, the writer lacks perseverance and needs outside pressure to fulfil the tasks he sets out to do. If the first and last letter or words are emphasized, combined with sharp pressure and illegible formations, beware! Such a writer is thoughtless, ungrateful and tactless.

A compass is a handy gadget to help establish the variation of sizes within a writing. Measure the size of letters with a compass and ruler. If your findings vary greatly and the writing is uneven, this means the writer is not very stable. He is a moody sort, someone who doesn't find it easy to steer an even course.

If illegibility occurs in a large writing, a sense of detail will be lacking. Unrhythmical changes of slant and wavy lines indicate a person who has been thrown out of gear by adverse circumstances. If other findings confirm this, the illegibility may also indicate insincerity or deceit, or at the very least a wish to conceal the truth. Someone who changes his letter formation frequently within whatever he is writing is either very versatile — if the writing is of a generally high standard — or else if the writing is of a low standard, lacking in principles.

Positive/negative

It is important when assessing personal qualities and characteristics from handwriting to decide whether the writing is positive or negative. This comes from an overall impression rather than individual items. The first impression is important, since other items you investigate may also fall into a more negative or positive place as you go along. It rarely happens that the first impression is not confirmed in further analysis.
Positive or negative assessment makes a great difference to your interpretation — for instance, narrow writing with firm pressure can mean initiative, ambition and self-possession, all very positive qualities. On the other hand, a negative script will turn the interpretation towards 'negative' traits, in this case recklessness, lack of self-control or impatience. Strictly speaking there is no such thing as absolutely positive or negative writing: but since one needs some standard or ruling from which to work, the following is a useful guideline.

Positive writing

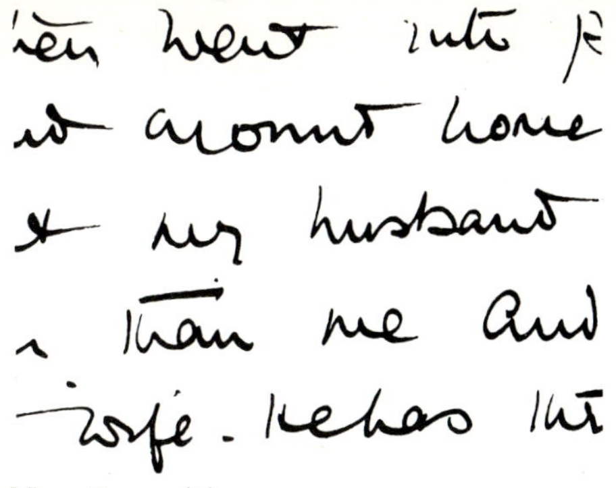

Negative writing

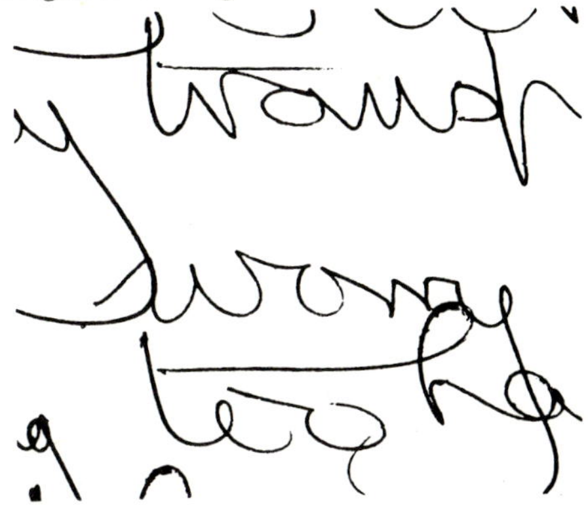

Positive writing

Positive writing fulfils its purpose first of all as a means of communication by being legible. It uses the writing space neatly. The margins and the spaces between lines are such that they form a pattern which is easy to read. The deviations from the school model mean that legibility is not impaired, and the writing is speeded up. The zones are harmoniously proportioned and the whole script is a pleasure to see and read.

Negative writing

On the other hand a negative script shows odd discrepancies at first glance. The lines probably intermingle and letter formations are badly shaped, leaving one in doubt as to which letter they actually represent. The size of letters is often exaggerated — either extremely large or small, making comprehension difficult, if not impossible. Margins and spacings are disorderly, and the whole document has an unpleasing appearance.

Capitals

Capital letters are of special interest to a graphologist because they form the size and shape of the upper zone. They are based, of course, on the line which forms the middle zone, but they should only go up into the upper zone. Since we are concerned mainly with writing in English, we must consider the fact that capitals are more rare than they are in other languages. On the other hand English is the only language in which the first person 'I' — the writer, the self, or ego — has a capital letter at all times, not only at the beginning of a sentence.

First person 'I'

It is possible to tell quite a lot about a writer from the way the 'I' is shaped, both in size and formation. If the 'I' is much larger than any other capital letter, you can assume that the writer has — or at least pretends to have — a high opinion of himself. If it is markedly smaller, the opposite is the case. A well-adjusted, harmonious person who is content with his role within society writes a letter which is in equal proportion to the rest of the writing.

Illegible capitals

If intelligent writers speed up the writing progress they try to streamline their capital letters. This can go too far, of course, and the writing becomes difficult to read.
It is also possible to enrich capital letters beyond recognition. This may not render the script unreadable, but it slows the speed of writing down, because any unnecessary movement must cause delay.
Anything which seriously reduces the speed of writing means that the writer is either inefficient or hesitant or lacking good judgement and taste. He may be suffering from all these things. He may also need to underline his difference from others or to make an impact on the society within which he lives. Whether this is a clever, efficient or even effective way of doing so is another matter. It is necessary to find out what makes people write in the way they do and why may they feel the need to make a particular impression on their society? These things will become clear after other features are analyzed.

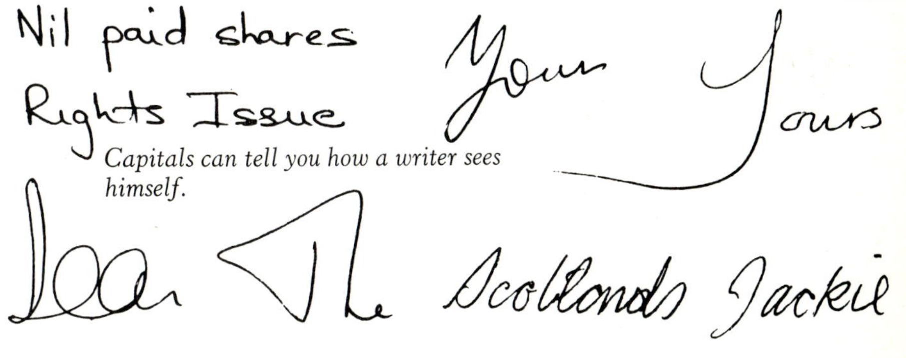

Capitals can tell you how a writer sees himself.

i-dots and t-bars

The letters 'i' and 't' are the only two letters which are the same in every school model, regardless of nationality. This is a great help to any graphologist who is asked to analyze a manuscript written in a language he cannot understand.

i-dots

The dot over the 'i' can be low or high, ahead of the letter or just a little to the left. The slant of the writing and its interpretation are important here.

Backward-slanting script A low-placed dot to the left of the stem shows a very cautious person. If the dot is where it belongs exactly above the stem, we still find caution, but also a good retentive memory and attention to detail. If the dot is placed low and to the right, caution is combined with desire for action, an urge to get things moving. Dots placed in a relatively high position combine caution with an enquiring mind. When the dot is placed exactly on top, but high — which is quite a difficult thing to do — it spells accuracy, imagination and a more constructive degree of caution and inquisitiveness. When the dot is high, and in advance of the letter, discretion is shown. With this goes an enquiring mind and a measure of imagination and vision.

Upright script A low dot slightly to the left shows a writer who is a little cautious, but independent in judgement; he may be a practical realist. If the dot is placed on top of the letter, one finds an accurate person, who has good, practical judgement. If the dot is far to the right, it shows an active mind with vision and realism. If the dot is high to the left, the writer will reserve his final decision. When the dot is correctly placed on top of the stem, a shrewd combination of planning, movement and action exists, and all unnecessary reserve has been overcome.

Forward-slanting script A low-placed dot to the left of the stem indicates a writer who has learned to brake a little before he rushes into action. If the dot is on top, a positive, realistic and well-balanced writer is at work. A low dot ahead of the letter comes from an impatient person of extreme action. He is a realist with constructive vision; he may be in a top position in industry. High dots on the left are a positive sign, since the dot's cautionary position indicates that this writer is someone who takes note of everything that is going on without hindering progress. If it is high and forward, the writer has forward vision and imagination.

t-bars

The t-bar can be just as informative as the i-dot. What is even more interesting is that a t-bar may occur in a capital T, as well as in a small 't'. Strong long bars are always indicative of leadership of some sort, and short ones show a tendency toward subordination.

Some i-dots

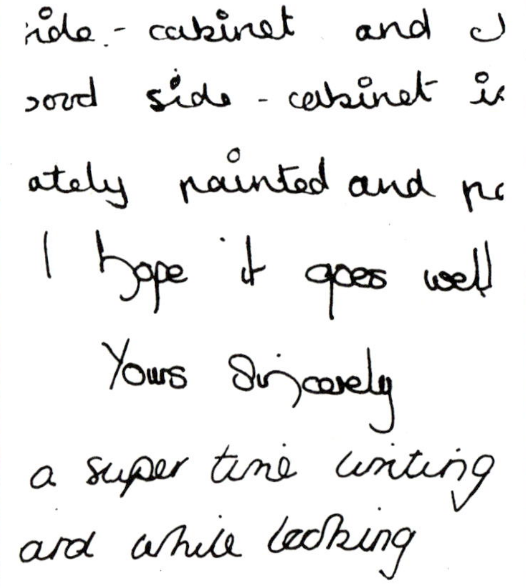

Different t-bars

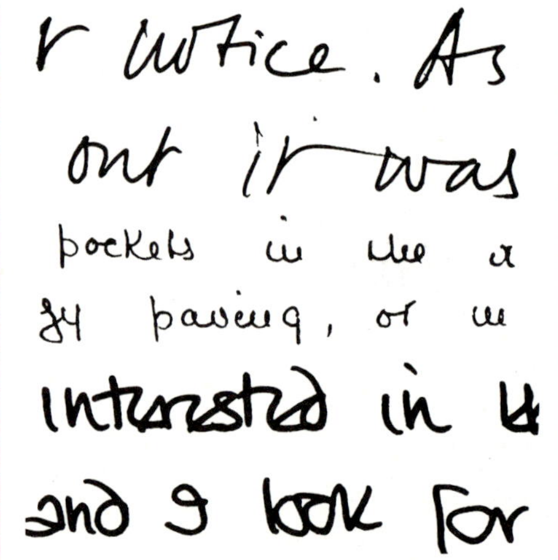

The position of t-bars is interpreted in the same way as i-dots, but it is no longer necessary to point out what each slant of the writing indicates.

Left-hand placing A low-placed bar indicates uncertainty and possibly feelings of inferiority. If the bar is raised to the middle of the stem caution is shown. If the stroke is on the top, the writer has leadership potential but is too cautious to exercise his ability.

Central placing If the bar crosses the stem at the very bottom, the writer tries to overcome his feelings of inferiority by patiently and thoroughly following his duties. The correctly placed and shaped bar may come from a reliable and conscientious worker. A stroke which balances on top of the stem comes from a writer of leadership quality, who wishes to be in command or control, or to be recognized, but who may seek something outside his reach.

Right-hand placing A low short bar shows lack of confidence and reluctance to assume responsibility — the typical subordinate. A similar bar half way up still indicates lack of originality, but shows sufficient sense of responsibility to fulfil given duties carefully. If the stroke is at the top, but still short, the writer has limited leadership abilities.

A longish, but low-placed, bar shows a conscientious person who will be able to look after people working with, or under him. A long bar at the correct height shows an increased degree of responsibility. The writer is probably in a 'middle management' position. A high bar is a positive symbol of a writer who can control and supervise others correctly and fairly.

If the t-bar is woven into the first letter of the next word, forming a protective arm, we find a firm leader and manager, someone who likes problems to solve. He is quick in his decisions, does not waste time or energy, shows fine co-ordination and is meticulous. A zigzag bar shows an argumentative, quarrelsome person who likes to be right.

If the writer forgets to make any i-dots or t-strokes, he impairs the legibility of the writing. This may mean that he is not capable of accepting responsibility, since he lacks real purpose. Alternatively he may believe himself different from others and in this way demonstrates his refusal to conform to tradition and convention.

U.S. Presidents and their assassins

BETTMANN ARCHIVE

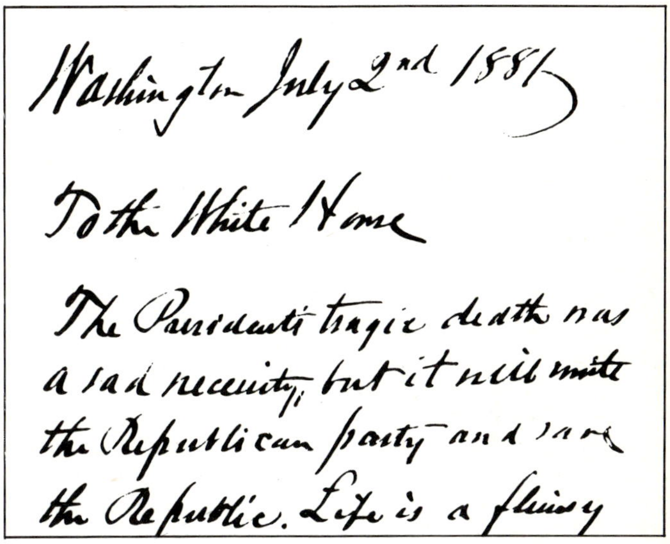

Washington July 2nd 1881

To the White House

The President's tragic death was
a sad necessity, but it will unite
the Republican party and save
the Republic. Life is a flimsy

The assassination of President Garfield of the United States in 1881: his signature is frank and pleasant in contrast to the spiteful script of Guiteau's confession.

BETTMANN ARCHIVE

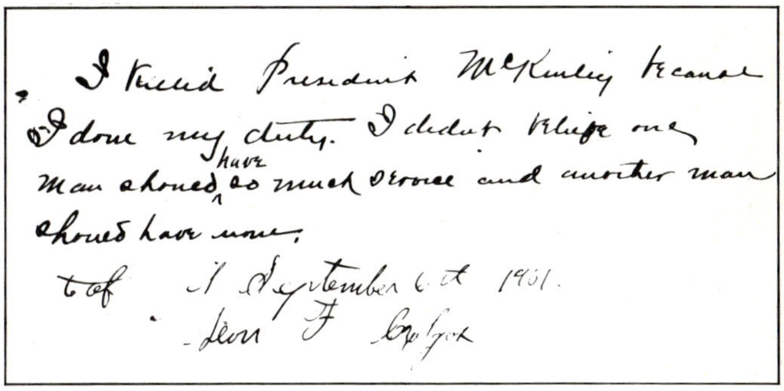

I killed President McKinley because
I done my duty. I didn't believe one
man should have so much service and another man
should have none.
6 of September 6th 1901.
Leon F Czolgosz

Compare the sincere, practical signature of President McKinley with the unbalanced script of Leon Czolgosz, who assassinated him in 1901.

Signatures

Like envelopes, signatures can also be strikingly different from the rest of the writing, both in size and letter formation. The signature is, in a manner of speaking, the visiting card of the writer, and the way it is written shows the impression that he wishes to make on the person he writes to, or on the world at large.

Legibility

Since writing in general should be legible if it is not to negate its purpose—communication—the signature should be legible too. But it rarely is. What can be deduced from this? Can it be that, for example, when someone signs a document which may contain a commitment in some form or other, he unconsciously hopes to 'leave the backdoor open' as an escape route? He could say, 'That doesn't say John Smith — it's just a scribble or doodle.' It may well be just that, but it is also a trade-mark of sorts, because nobody else can produce the same 'scribble or doodle'. Even if 'John Smith' hoped to get away with it, he certainly would not succeed, because handwriting experts would easily be able to identify the producer of the scribbles.

Types of signature

A large upper zone is often produced by people in business, particularly on the sales side, together with odd shapes in the lower zone.
Underlining, often combined with two dots underneath or one above and below the line, indicate that the signatory will stick to a bargain, making sure that every item of a contract is strictly kept. Lawyers, bankers, civil servants and people in similar professions often have this characteristic which is a sign of reliability and sincerity — provided the rest of their writing bears out the existence of these qualities.
Small signatures, smaller, that is, than the rest of the writing show modesty and even understatement.
Large signatures, on the other hand show that the writer is proud of his descent, position or success — or at least makes himself believe that he is.
Surnames and Christian names may be given different emphases. The surname is representative of the social element, and forms the nucleus of the signature, the whole Christian name or initials represent the private and intimate part of it. Children are exclusively called by their first names and the Christian name is therefore a symbol of 'childlikeness'. Wherever there is a harmonious balance and relationship between Christian-name and surname you can assume that there is no discord between private and public life. If the Christian name or initials are very much smaller than the rest of the signature, this is a sign that the writer is sacrificing his private life at the cost of position, power, success, and so on. If the first name is larger than the rest of the signature, this indicates that the importance of the writer's private life is so great to him that it over-rides all social considerations. If the Christian name slants to the left, in an otherwise differently directed signature, this shows an acute conflict between private and social life.
Signatures of married women are of special interest. A woman when she marries consents to take not only the man of her choice, but also his name, and her signature is a useful guide to her happiness, contentment, and satisfaction in married life. When she writes her Christian name or initial larger than the rest of the signature, it indicates that she was happier when unmarried. When her first name or initial is smaller than the next of the signature, the opposite is true. If surname and Christian name are the same size, the writer is well balanced and content. It must be pointed out in fairness that a husband's writing can be analyzed in a similar way; a man keeps his own surname of course, but if he writes his first name or initial, larger than his surname, he unconsciously feels that he was happier as a child or a bachelor. Bear this in mind if you ever find yourself in the position of marriage counsellor.

Opposite: All these signatures are from original specimens and are reproduced actual size. The majority are people who are, or have been, in the public eye, but four are ordinary people with quite different backgrounds. Two are British, one is from New Zealand, one from the United States. See if you can identify which is which!

Prince Rainier of Monaco A light-hearted, delightful hand. Humour, determination and an aloofness used to keep bores away. Pressure indicates determination, discipline and a high working capacity. I-dots are all-seeing eyes; he is firmly anchored to reality and material values. Strong powers of observation and well-disciplined.

Frank Harris Good pressure, combined with the size of the signature, indicate a man who knew his worth. He delivered the goods and did not mince words. He had a firm grasp of reality. He took no chances; everything was organized and down-to-earth. Self-loving and vain, but unashamedly honest about it.

George Bernard Shaw Small, cramped, legible. A man who had something to say, but who kept the public at arm's length. Upper zone is better developed than the lower, not in size but in loop-formation — intellect, not emotion inspired him. Size and crowding indicate a calculated generosity based on economic principles.

A very large, hasty signature with a long end-line putting a safe distance between him and the outside world. Here is a thoughtful but active man who knows what he wants and how to keep it when he gets it. The large loops show his imagination and depth of feeling. (John Ruck).

Here is an emotional person trying to find a way of life which promises fulfilment. Some letter formations indicate artistic discrimination. The neatly placed i-dots indicate a fine power of observation and a reliable factual memory. Some 'a' and 'o' formations are open, indicating that the writer is sincere, if a little blunt.

The writer is a fast worker and an imaginative thinker. The initial capitals intermingle and form a complex piece of abstract sculpture, which illustrates the complexity of his visions and his proclivity for doing more than one job at a time. (P. Edwards).

This signature shows a down-to-earth attitude to life. The slow, well-formed writing indicates reliability. Arcades and some disconnection show she thinks carefully over every step she takes. She is dependable, and intelligent, with common sense. (Jennifer T. Down).

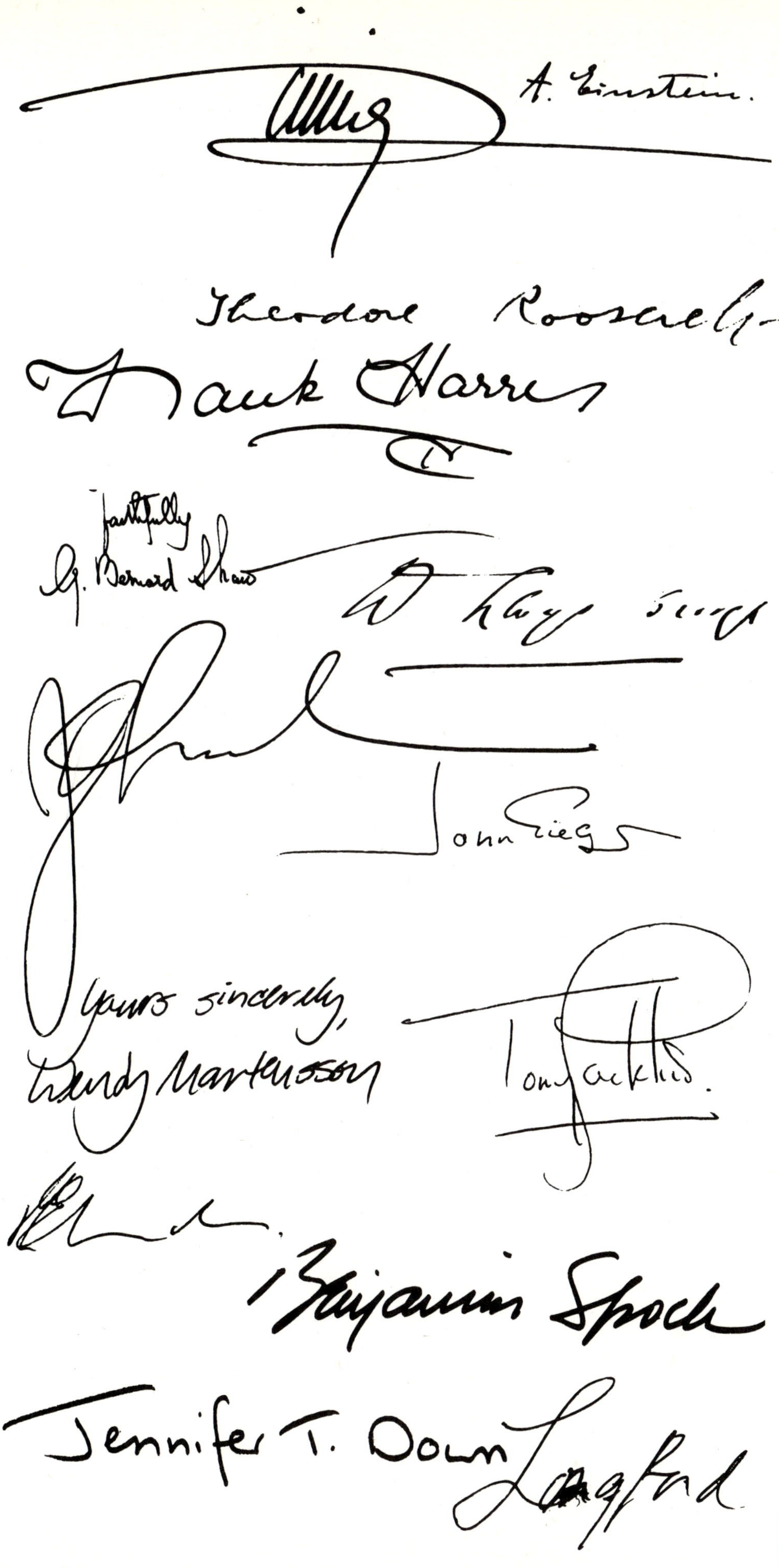

Albert Einstein Simple and childlike at first glance; but beautifully simplified. The garlanded capital 'E' in Einstein shows kindness and gentleness; angular connections indicate hard, concentrated work confirmed by the first low i-dot. The high t-bar indicates that he knew his degree of authority, but innate modesty held him in check.

Theodore Roosevelt Sensitive, well-shaped writing with pressure, indicating energy and mental prowess. Letter formations are unassuming, clear and legible. The wide space between Christian name and surname indicates the breathing space he needed to formulate his thoughts. Honest and sincere, free from vanity.

Lloyd George Highly intelligent, well underlined to boost his self-respect, but with delicate line-connection. Speed and pressure show intuition and intellectual shrewdness. Everything is brought to bare essentials. The downstroke and pressure indicate his ability to get things done, with time for thought and meditation.

John Gielgud A highly intelligent man with great powers of concentration. I-dots indicate reliable memory. His signature is larger than the rest of his writing, showing modest pride in his success. He likes to impress his fellow men.

Tony Jácklin The letter 'J' aims for a hole in one! Slight, firm pressure indicates discipline and concentration; lines over and under show that he is aware of his obligations. A hook at the first t-bar — and right hand underlining — show an ability to cope with reality. He is well-balanced and confident.

Dr. Benjamin Spock A man who makes an impact. An idealist; honest; no-one interferes with his ideas. Well educated. 'j' and 'i' dots indicate a quick mind that thinks ahead. The capital 'S' and small 'p' show ability to plan and organize. Copes with reality cautiously — note the closed 'a' and 'o'. Angular connections show conviction.

Lord Longford Well-shaped, large, intelligently simplified and legible. A man whose superior intelligence concentrates on basics. The end curve of his signature indicates a gentle man who does not bear grudges. A rational pride is shown in the large 'L', and the 'g'. Personal matters take second place to public life.

How to analyze a sample

By this time you have a foundation and understanding of the theory of graphology. Now you can apply this knowledge to the analysis of any sample of handwriting, using the step-by-step analysis section which follows. Carefully evaluate every aspect of the writing according to the questions, writing down the number and letter which applies (i.e. if the writing slopes slightly backwards, the key will be 11a). If the question does not apply, leave it out. It will not make any difference to the final analysis.

Equipment

Certain equipment is necessary to begin a thorough analysis. It is always easier to do the job — be it woodworking, dressmaking or sheep-shearing — if the proper tools are at hand. You will need the following:
a pad and pencil for note taking; a compass; a protractor; a ruler; an orange stick, toothpick or sharpened matchstick; tracing paper. (You may find it easier to trace the diagrams and place them directly on to the sample when assessing angles, zones, space between lines, etc.)

Before you start

There are certain facts to ascertain before you begin.
Nationality As we have seen, school models vary widely and must be taken into account immediately.
Age Characteristics of aging can appear in the writing of younger people with various illnesses.
Sex We are all bi-polar rather than bi-sexual, which means that men have some feminine characteristics and women are masculine to some degree. Make sure the characteristics you find are really indicative or just appear occasionally. Some writing is fairly standard so try not to read eccentricities into it! Many letters can be made in a variety of ways in a single piece of writing so look for the majority and interpret from that.
When you have completed the questions, key all the numbers to the relevant answers. Do not be tempted to look at the answers until you have completed the full analysis — it may influence your final interpretation. Check that you have not missed any combined characteristics which will add further points to your analysis.

Intuition

Do however play any hunch that may occur to you, based on prior knowledge of the writer or simply by putting clues together in a variety of ways. Although intuition is an un-scientific quality in a systematic method, it can be combined with knowledge and training. Intuition is a decisive factor in differentiating between a good technician and a brilliant one. The expert who clings to his textbook knowledge will never be outstanding.

The angle of lines

1 *Lay a ruler under the line of writing*
Is it straight and at right angles to the edge of the page?

2 **a)** Does it slope upwards—a little?
b) A lot?

a

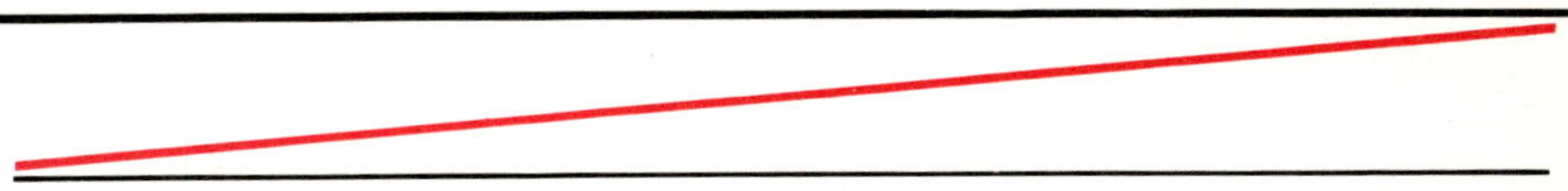

b

3 **a)** Does it slope downwards—a little?
b) A lot?

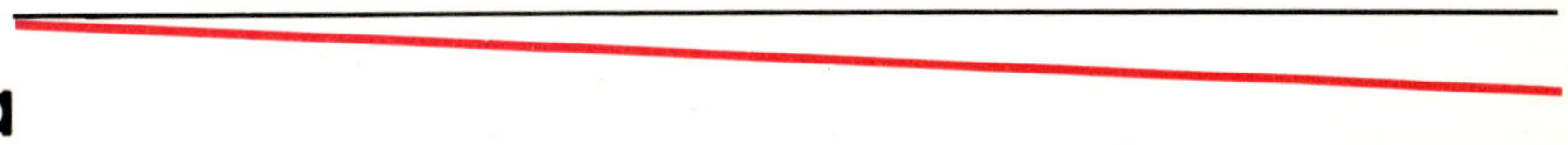

a

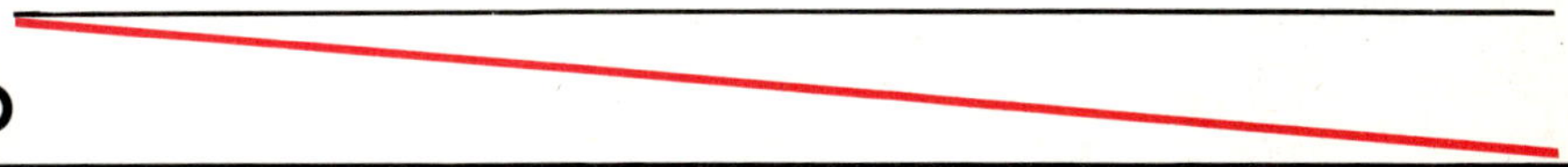

b

4 Does the line of writing wave up and down?

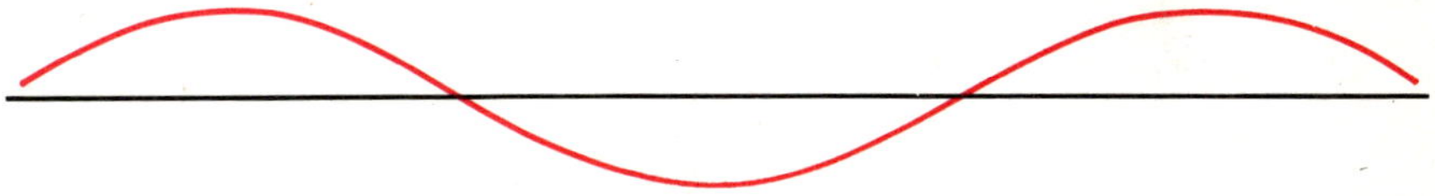

5 **a)** Does the line progress in steps up?
b) Or steps down?

a

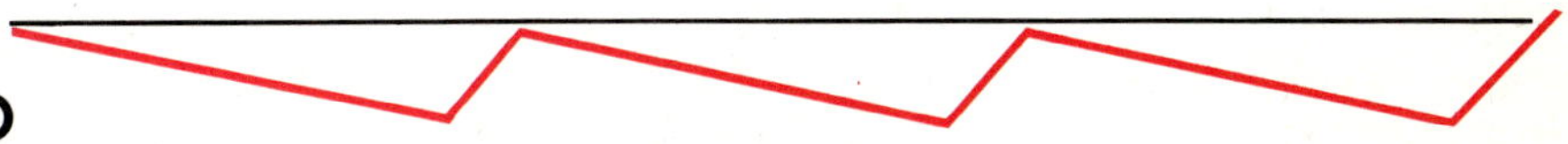

b

6 **a)** Does the writing arch in the middle?
b) Does it sag in the middle?

a

b

The three zones

7 How big is the middle zone?
a) Is it like this?
b) Or like this?
c) Or like this?
(Samples shown are twice life size.)

a middle zones

b middle zones

c middle zones

8 **a)** Are the middle zone letters evenly sized?
b) Do they start smaller and get larger?
c) Do they taper towards the end?
d) Are they uneven throughout?

b middle zones

c middle zones

d middle zones

9 **a)** Is the emphasis on the ascenders?
b) On the descenders?
c) Does the middle zone take precedence over both?

a straight and curved

b straight and curved

c straight and curved

The slant of the letters

10 Does the writing slope to the right?
a) A little?
b) A lot?

a

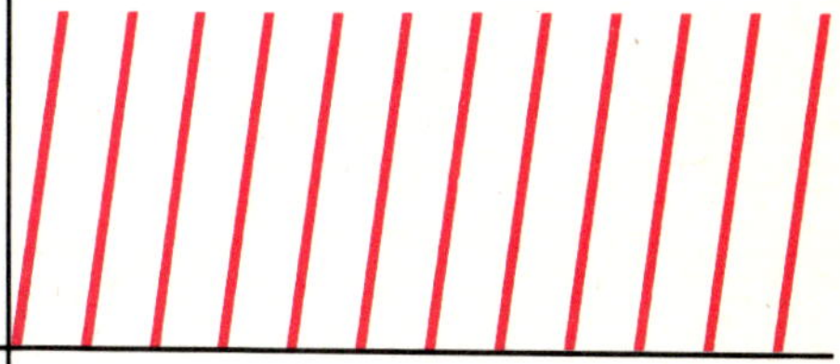

b

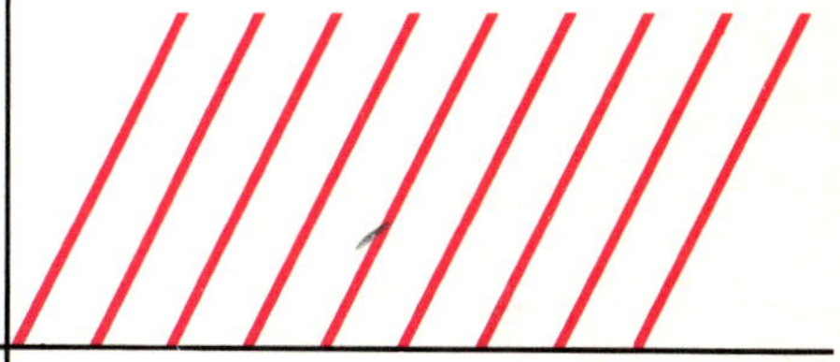

11 Does the writing slope to the left?
a) A little?
b) A lot?

a

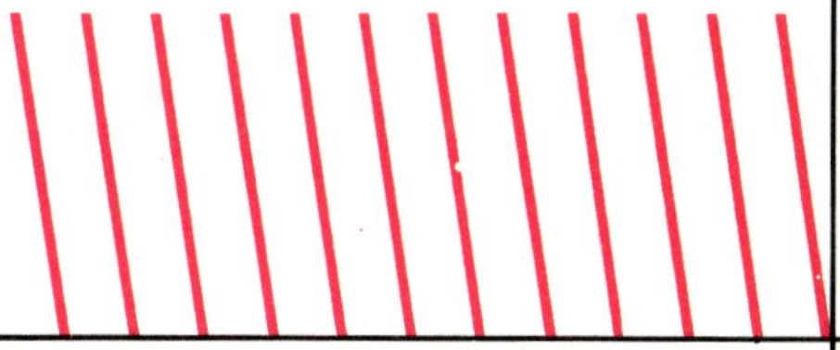

b

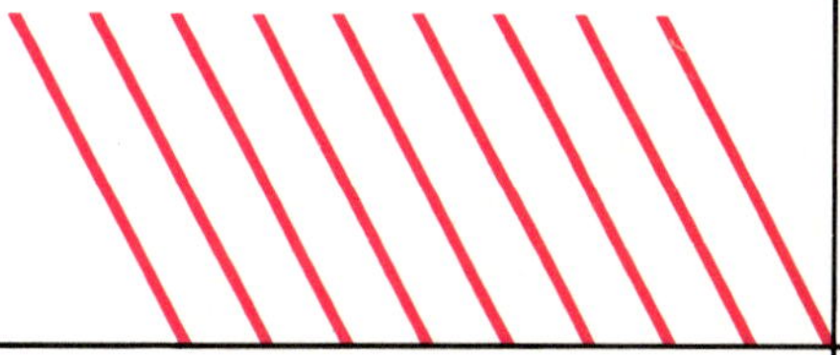

12 Is the writing upright?

Margins

13 If the margin is straight, how wide is it?
a) Narrow?
b) Medium, well-proportioned?
c) Wide?

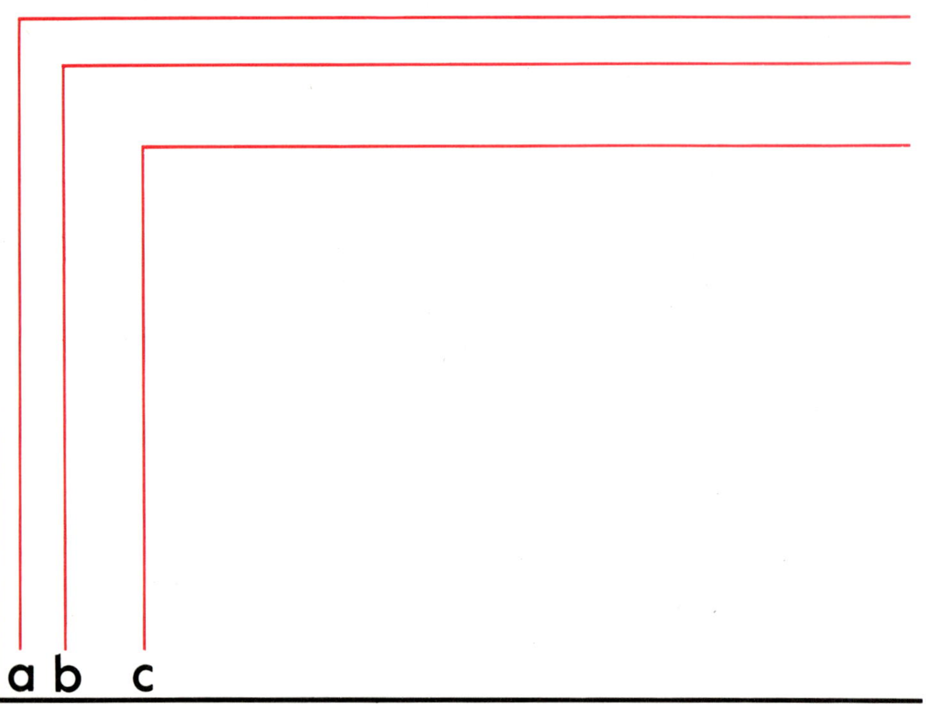

14 **a)** Does the left hand margin get wider towards the bottom?
b) Or narrower?

15 Is the left hand margin missing altogether?

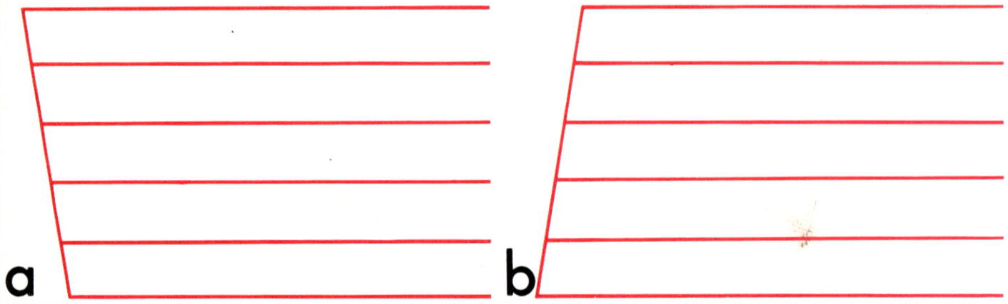

16 Is the left hand margin uneven?
a) Jerky, in steps?
b) Wavy?

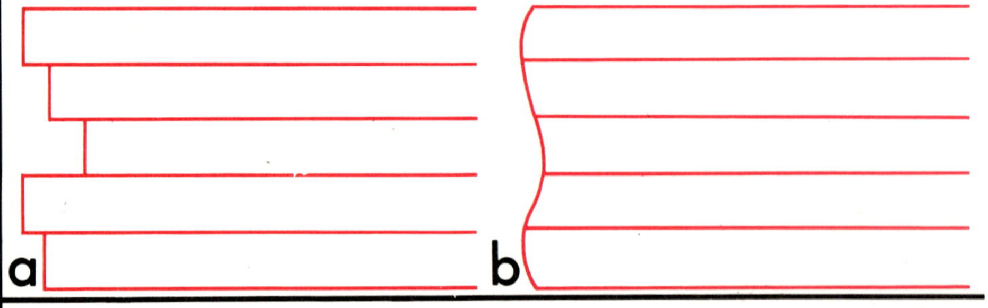

17 Is the right hand margin
a) Unnaturally regular?
b) Naturally uneven, but well spaced to indicate a margin?
c) Or do words 'drop over the edge' or have to be squeezed in?

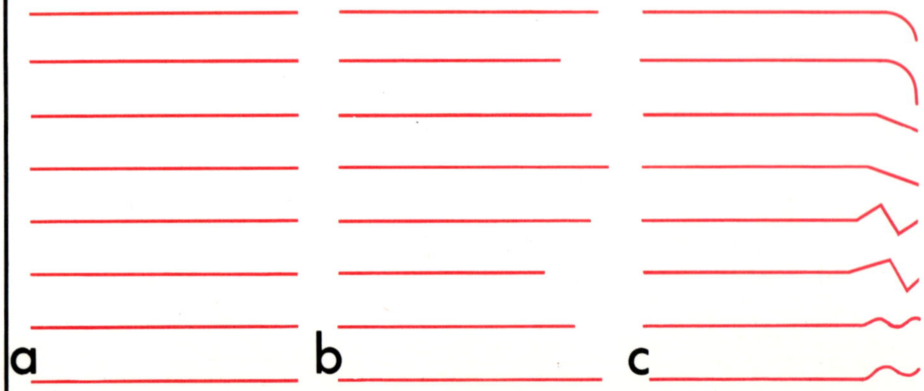

Space between lines

18 How well spaced are the lines?

a) Are they so close together that letters touch or mix?
b) Quite close but not touching?
c) Clearly spaced?
d) Very widely spaced?

Envelopes

19 *If the writing you are analyzing came in an envelope written at the same time, apply these questions to the envelopes.*

a) Is the address positioned in the centre?
b) Very high?
c) Very low?
d) Far left?
e) Far right?

20 **a)** Is the writing the same as the main script?
b) Is it illegible?
c) Is it larger than the main script?
d) Is it smaller?

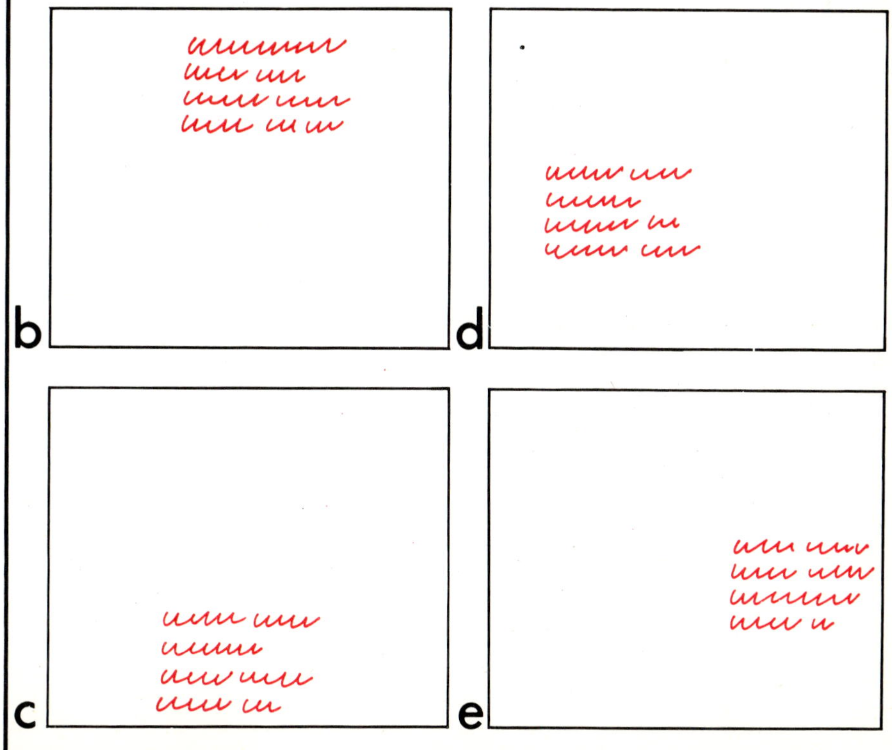

How letters are joined

21 *Work out which type of connection predominates.*

a) Are the connections garlanded like this?
b) Or arcades like this?
c) Angular like this?
d) Or threads like this?

a garlands

b arcades

c angular

d threads

22 **a)** Are the connections spread out like this?
b) Close together like this?

a wide apart

b close together

23 **a)** Are some of the letters disconnected, like this?
b) Are they all disconnected?

a some disconnected

b all disconnected

The width of the writing

24 *Measure the extension of the letters, using only the middle zone.*

a) Are the letters very close and cramped like this?
b) Are they wide like this?
c) Are they quite regular like this?

a close and cramped

b wide like this

c regular

Pressure

25 How much pressure does the writing show?

a) Is it fine and spidery?
b) Is it firm and even?
c) Is it heavy?

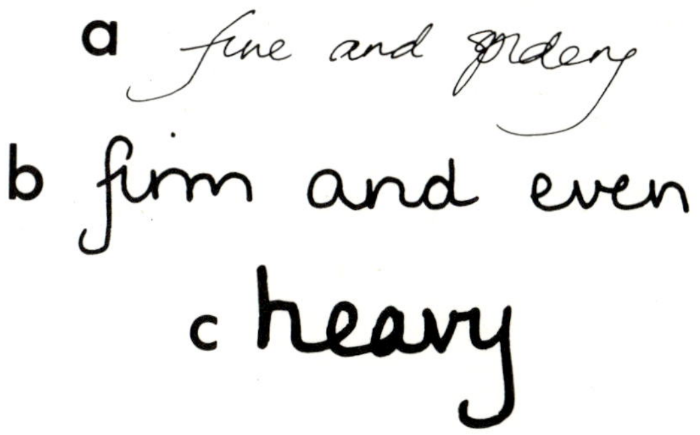

26 **a)** Does the writing have conscious thick and thin lines, done for effect?
b) Is it irregularly thick and thin?
c) Is it consistently thick and pasty?

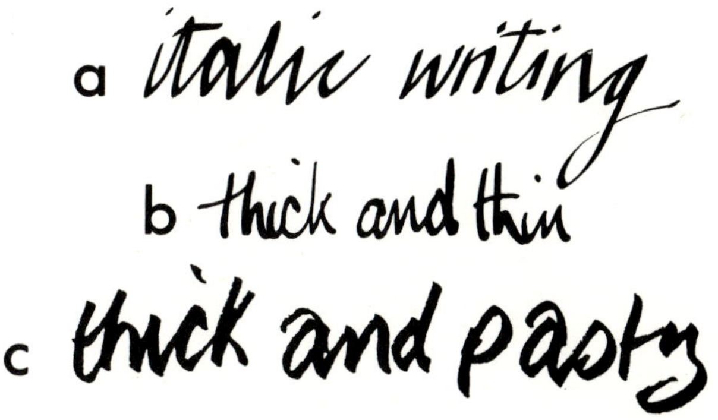

Speed and rhythm

27 *Follow the writing with an orange stick to feel the flow and rhythm.*

a) Is the rhythm very smooth and quick?
b) Is it slow and careful?
c) Is it jerky or disjointed?
d) Is it hasty so that some words are illegible?

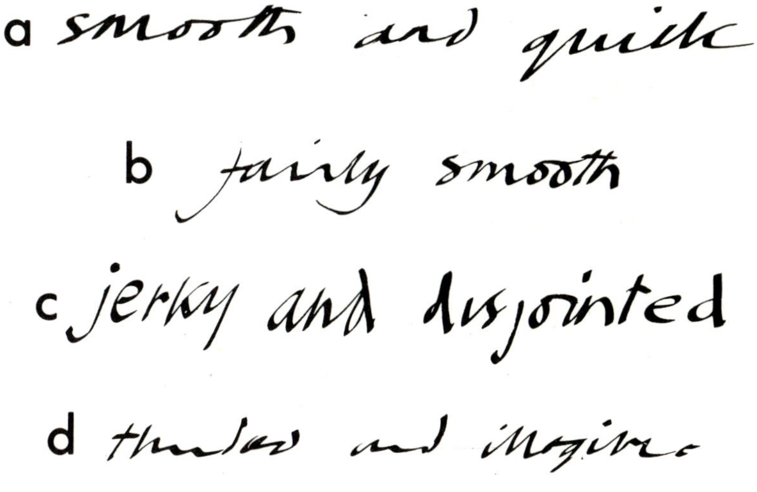

Initials and finals

28 a) Do words begin with long straight strokes like these?
b) With a garlanded first stroke?
c) An arcaded first stroke?
d) Do they start with enrichments like these?

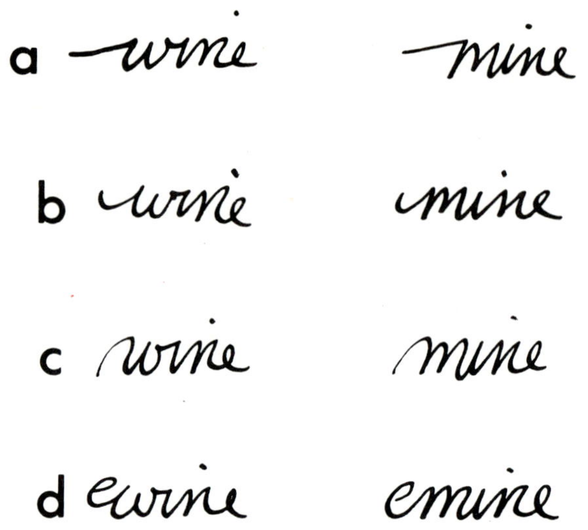

29 a) Do end-strokes point to the right like these?
b) Are they clipped like these?
c) Do they go up in arcades like these?
d) Do words finish with garlands like these?

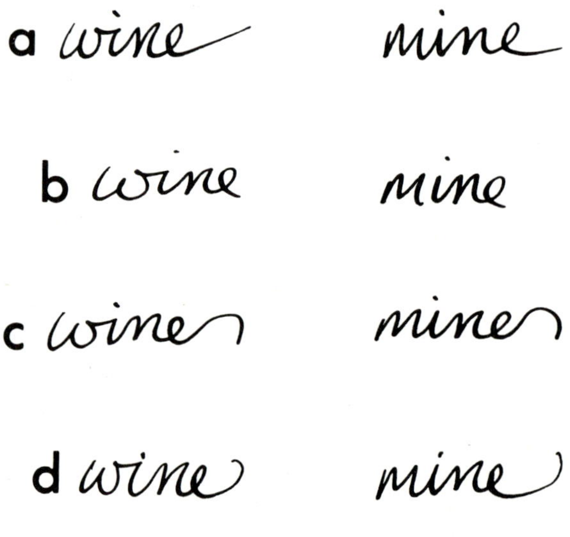

Words joined by finals

30 Are words joined together?
a) Never
b) Occasionally
c) Nearly every word

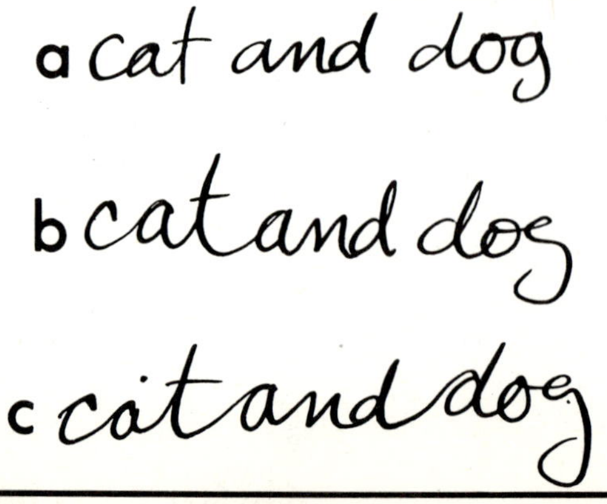

Dr Manfred Lowengard, the author of this book, likes to spend many hours poring over a specimen of writing. To him a magnifying glass is vitally important, so that he can catch the minute changes of emphasis in every single stroke of the pen.

Capital letters

31 How do capitals relate to the middle zone?

- **a)** Are they low?
- **b)** Quite standard?
- **c)** Are they high like this?
- **d)** Are they embellished?

First person 'I'

32 Are the first person 'I's like any of the following? (Remember to look for the majority if the formations vary.)

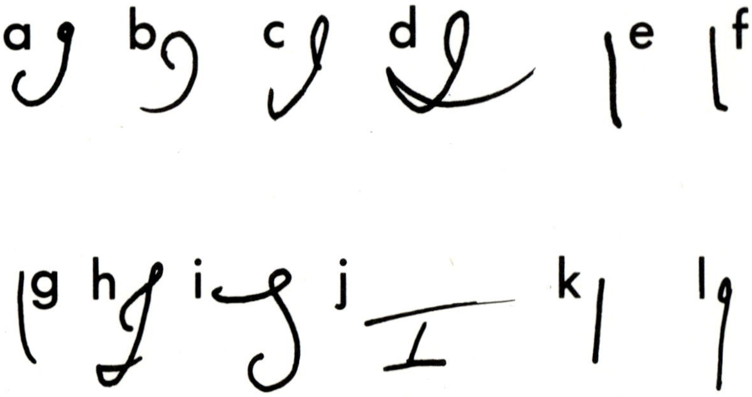

Simple and ornate

33 **a)** Does the writing include awkward embellishments like this?
b) No embellishments at all?
c) Creative embellishments which add style to the writing?

a

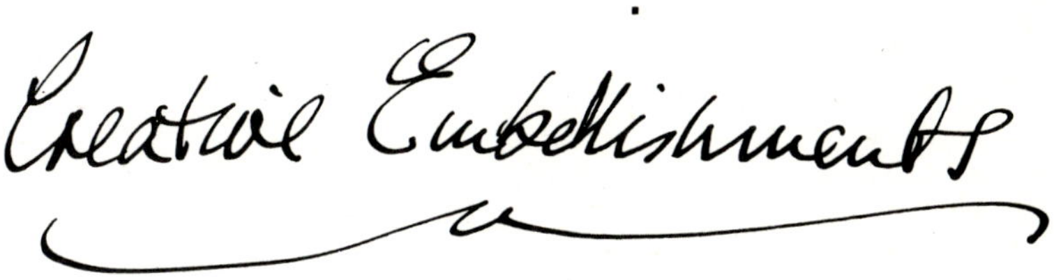

c

34 **a)** Do simplifications help the speed and clarity of the writing?
b) Are all letters simplified so much that their meaning is not always clear?

a

b

Signatures

35 Does the signature differ from the main writing in any of the following ways:
a) Is it larger?
b) Is it smaller?
c) Is it less legible?
d) Is it just as legible?
e) Is it more embellished?

a

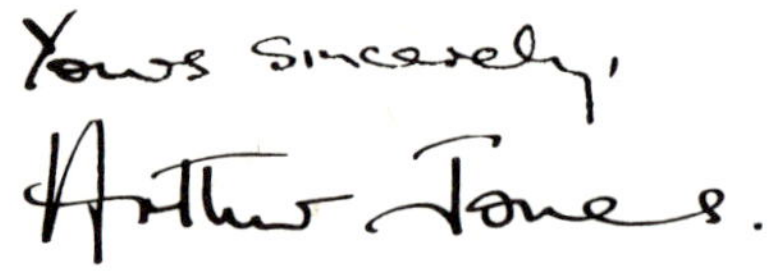

b

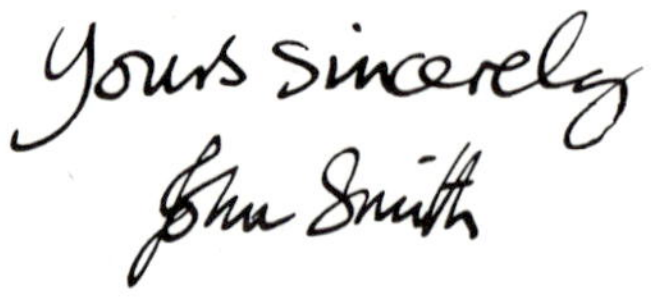

c

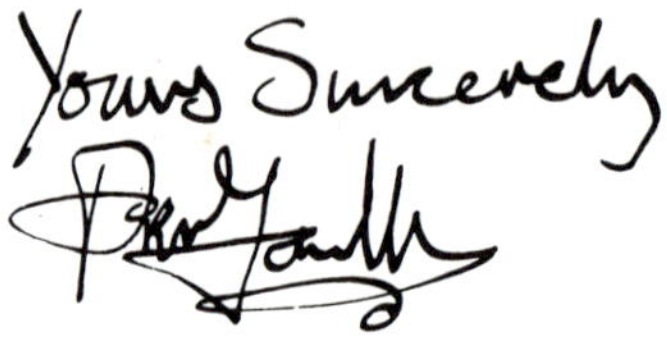

d

e

36 **a)** Is there a full stop at the end?
b) Is it underlined?

a

b

37 **a)** Is the first (Christian) name or initial more emphasized than the surname?
b) Is it less emphasized?
c) Is there an equal emphasis?

a

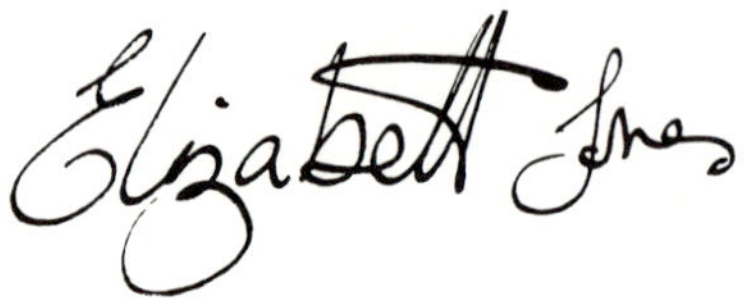

b

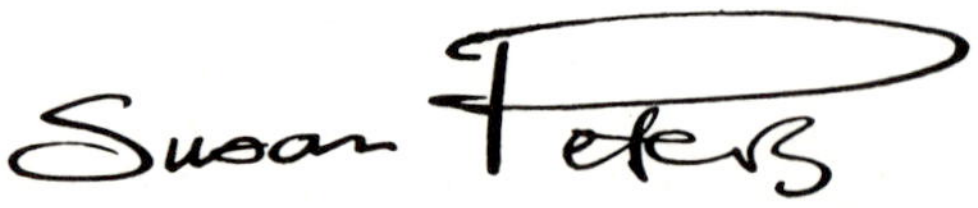

c

Letter formations

38 **a)** Are the 'a' and 'o' letters open at the top? **b)** Are some of them open? **c)** Are they open at the bottom? **d)** Are they all closed? **e)** Are the 'o's knotted at the top?	a open b Some open c open d all closed e knotted
39 Are the tails of letters open (i.e., made of 2 strokes)?	
40 Bearing in mind questions 8, 26 and 29, are the ascenders **a)** Looped like this? **b)** Simplified like this?	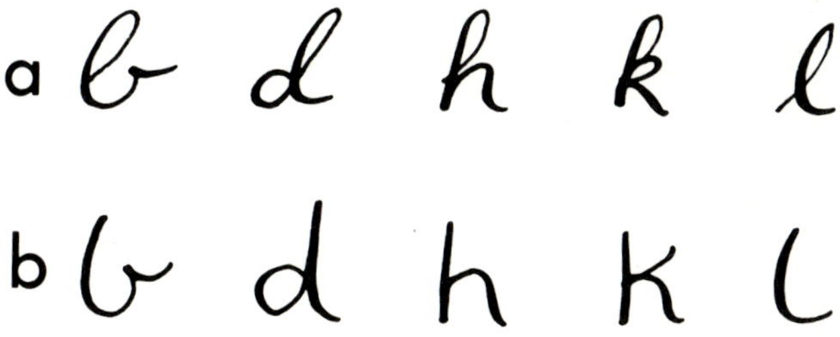
41 Are the 'd's and 'e's 'Greek' formations like this?	
42 Are the descenders of these letters **a)** Looped like this (including 'z' in some school models)? **b)** Curved like this? **c)** With flourished loops like this? **d)** Or like this? **e)** Are the descenders straight, with neither loops nor curves?	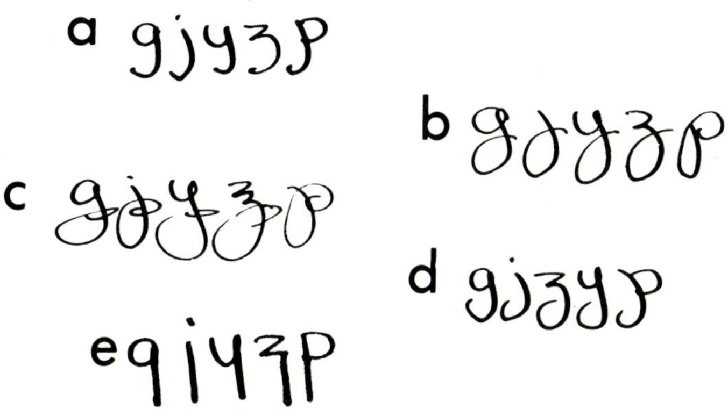
43 Are 'l' or 's' formations crossed through like pound or dollar signs?	

44 *Note the position of the i-dots. Bear in mind questions 9, 10 and 11.*

a) Is the i-dot directly above the stem?
b) To the right?
c) To the left?
d) Is it heavy?
e) Faint?
f) A dash or tick?
g) A circle?
h) High?
i) Low?
j) Omitted altogether?

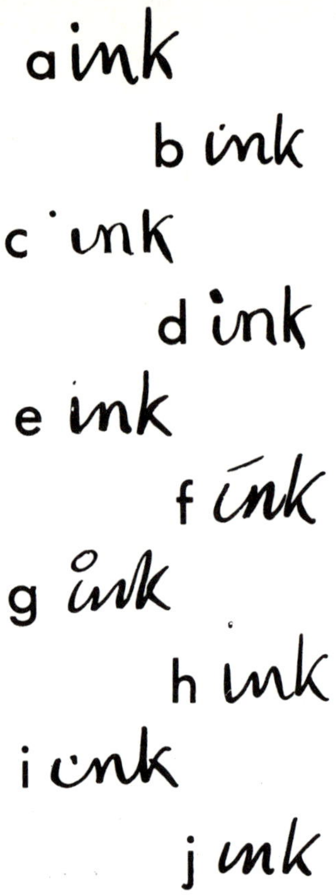

45 *Note the position of the t-bars. These are related closely to the position of the i-dots.*

a) Do the t-bars cross the stem like this?
b) Or like this?
c) Are they to the right like this?
d) Or like this?
e) Are they to the left?
f) Are they faint?
g) Or heavy?
h) Are they high?
i) Or low?
j) Do they slant up?
k) Or down?
l) Are they knotted?
m) Do the finals form the cross?
n) Are the t-bars above the stem?
o) Are they long enough to cover the whole word, or used as a connection?
p) Are they omitted?
q) Do they curve over the stem?
r) Do they curve over a very short stem?

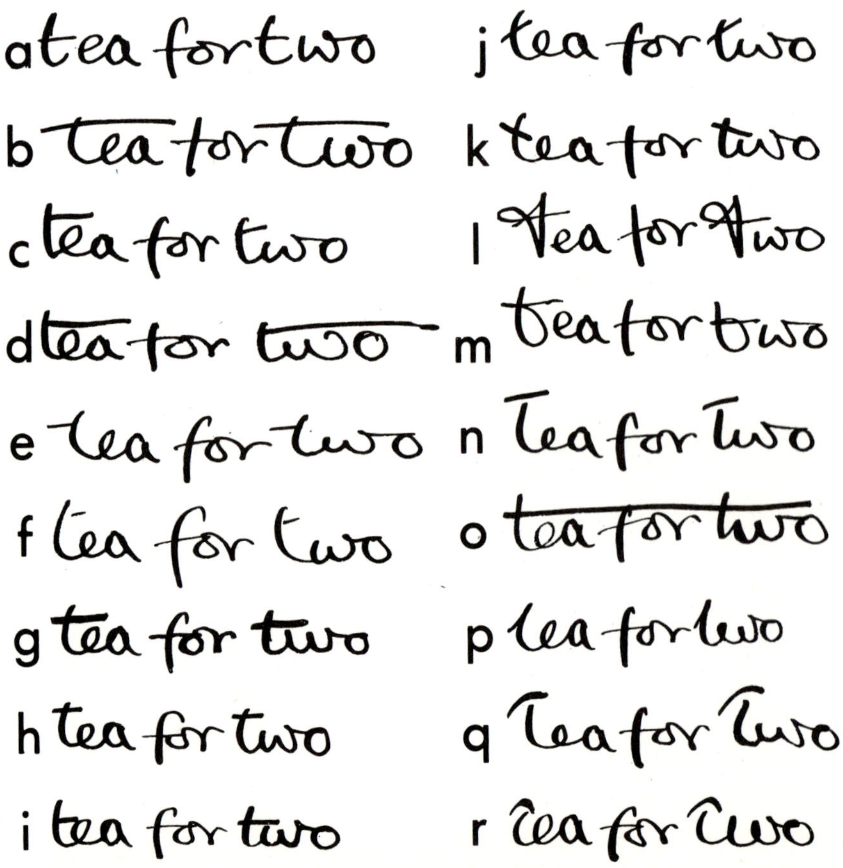

All the answers

1. Toeing the line. Conventional. Reliable.

2. a) Active, positive writer who knows his aims and ambitions.
b) Too anxious to succeed. Perhaps a little hasty in judgement. Optimistic.

3. a) Fatigue. Slight depression. Worry that problems are too much to cope with.
b) Depressive. Physical or mental fatigue. Pessimism.

4. Emotional. Slightly unstable.

5. a) and **b)** Writer is trying to control undue optimism or pessimism, depending on whether the lines go up in steps or down.

6. a) Enthusiasm held in check.
b) Either fatigue or depression held in check.
In other words both denote self-control.

7. a) This is the average size of most writing and means little on its own: it could mean thoroughness, convention, honesty, loyalty or even possessiveness.
b) Pride, vanity, ambition, pretention, enterprise, arrogance, self-esteem, enthusiasm, excitability. Very large writing shows a tendency towards irritability.
c) Power to concentrate; conscientiousness; critical, analytical mind: often an academic, whether literary or scientific.

8. a) Another sign of a conscientious nature.
b) Tactless.
c) Diplomacy, discretion, tact. A good businessman.
d) Keeps his feelings to himself, but can be moody. In a strong personality could be objective and observant.

9. a) Idealism; ambition; intuition.
b) Sensualist; exaggeration; materialist.
c) An over-developed ego — a tendency to throw his weight about and influence others.

10. a) Keenness, optimism, will to succeed.
b) Emotions may run away with the writer. Lack of self control.

11. a) The writer is not too keen to face the future.
b) Cautious, unapproachable. Could have something of a mother complex — or a hankering for the past.

12. This can be considered as a slight leftward movement when the writer's school model slopes to the right. If an upright school model was used and this is adhered to, it indicates self-control, reticence, or general lack of emotion. Poise, coolness and an ability to weigh up people and situations.

13. a) A sign of practical economy — not necessarily meanness, but the wish to get as much information on to the page as possible.
b) The normal margin which means nothing by itself.
c) A very wide left-hand margin show the writer's desire to put a safety margin between himself and his objective. If both margins are wide it shows culture or good taste.

14. a) If the left-hand margin gets wider towards the bottom it shows an affectionate nature. It also shows some extravagance, especially with money — inability to save.
b) Margins getting narrower show practical money sense.

15. No margins at all show neurosis, self-obsession with no room for anyone else's feelings.

16. a) A bad organizer, talkative, a

Combined characteristics

Many of the answers given above and overleaf are modified when combined with others. For instance, even-sized middle zone letters [**8a**] *combined with i-dots directly over their stems* [**44a**] *show a painstaking nature.*

Double check your answers and see if any of these combinations apply to the writing you are analyzing.

4. Wavy lines in an otherwise quick, [**27a**] garlanded [**21a**] script with neat margins show willingness to try anything once and do the best he can. Wavy lines combined with several changes of slant show a person thrown out of step by adverse circumstances.

7. a) Average-sized writing combined with clearly spaced lines [**18c**], neat margins or angular connections [**21c**] means a good head for business.
c) Combined with hooked finals [**29d**] and narrow letters [**24a**] can indicate niggling or petty attention to detail.

Combined with drooping lines [**3b**] it indicates depression and a feeling of inferiority.

8. a) Combined with i-dots placed directly above [**44a**], painstaking.
b) Writing which increases in size in forward-sloping writing [**10b**] indicates moral zeal.

c) Combined with straight lines [**1**] or small writing [**7c**]: versatility.
Combined with leftward t-bars [**45e**]: or faint t-bars [**45f**]; a sign of chronic indecision.

9. c) Combined with large size [**7b**] this writer has problems in coping with everyday matters.

11. b) Combined with any of the following, it indicates brutality: a medium-sized middle zone [**7a**]; heavy pressure [**25d**]; uneven middle zone letters [**8d**]; heavy t-bars [**45g**].

12. Combined with angular connections [**21c**] this can show laziness or indolence.
Combined with very small writing [**7c**] or hooked finals [**29d**]: avarice.
Combined with thick t-bars [**45g**] or

All the answers

restless mind.
b) Absent-minded.

17. a) Another sign of neurosis: an obsessive love of order and self-control, even inhibition.
b) This is normal and shows a well-balanced, easy-going personality, with a sense of order and style.
c) A talkative person, with little feeling for time.

18. a) Confusion to the point of unbalance — it is very jumbled. Indifference to luxury.
b) This is normal and shows ability to sort out ideas.
c) Clear and logical.
d) Isolation.

19. a) This is normal.
b) This indicates a dreamer.
c) Clings to the material and practical side of relationships.
d) Shy, unforthcoming.
e) Extrovert, dependent on others.

20. a) An unaffected person who has no desire to appear other than he is.
b) Someone who finds it difficult to adapt, is tactless or clumsy socially.
c) Self-assurance which is a pose — lack of sincerity.
d) The writer's self-confidence is greater than his somewhat reserved outward behaviour might appear.

21. a) Impressionable, receptive nature.
b) Reserve, conservatism.
c) Resilience, strength, perseverance; possibly dogmatic attitudes.
d) Flexible, changeable, easily influenced; fast-thinking.

22. a) Spontaneity, expansiveness.
b) Restraint, moderation.

23. a) A good judge of character. A person who relies partly on logic, partly on intuition.
b) Another sign of isolation, probably due to absent-mindedness or an impractical nature.

24. a) Restraint, moderation.
b) Wasteful, careless.
c) Drive and spontaneity.

25. a) Sensitivity, refinement, spirituality, modesty.
b) Energy, elasticity. This is average.
c) A strong but rigid will, obstinate.

26. a) Affection and conventionality, especially if the writing is close to the school model.
b) An insistent character, with a forceful personality.
c) Sensuality, voluptuousness, brutality.

27. a) Spontaneity, drive, action, an ambitious personality.
b) Deliberate nature, thorough.
c) Inhibition, frustration, dissatisfaction.
d) Lack of method, rashness.

28. a) Obstinate, stubborn.
b) Genuine, open, welcoming nature.
c) Polite, conventional.
d) Hesitant, bad judgement.

29. a) Generous nature.
b) Selfishness or reticence; disappointment.
c) An open but spiritual nature.
d) Dogmatic attitudes.

30. a) This is normal and means little on its own.
b) Speed and quick thinking.
c) Talkative, a busybody.

31. a) Modesty, a humble nature, simplicity.
b) This is normal and means little on its own.
c) Self-respect, conceit. The higher the capitals the more conceited the writer.
d) Affection, vanity, an overblown idea of self-importance.

32. a) Well-balanced, humble.

Combined characteristics

embellished capital letters [**31d**]: arrogance.

13. a) Combined with small, narrow writing [**7c, 24a**] it is a sign of thrift.
c) Combined with large writing [**7b**], this shows wastefulness or extravagance.

15. Neurosis is especially confirmed if non-existent margins are combined with arcaded [**21b**] or angled connections [**21c**].

19. c) Combined with drooping lines [**3b**] this means that the writer is easily depressed by practical difficulties.

21. a) and **b)** Arcades combined with garlands denote secretiveness. If the garlands are obviously mechanical — following the school model very correctly — it shows reserve or hypocrisy.
d) Threads in small writing [**7c**] show hypersensitivity. If only the ends of the words deteriorate this shows lack of perseverance.

22. a) If the letters are very wide apart, with wide spaces between lines [**18d**], this can mean isolation and lack of spontaneity.
Wide writing with firm pressure [**25c**] can show initiative, ambition or recklessness and impatience. With light pressure [**25a**], it shows tolerance, imagination, adventurousness, superficiality. Look for other signs to decide which applies.
b) Narrow writing with firm pressure [**25b**], can show moderation, tact, discipline, reserve, or even jealousy, distrust, or deceit. With light pressure, [**25a**] it shows caution, timidity, anxiety, narrowmindness.

b) Sensitive, nervous.
c) Keen, ambitious.
d) Down-to-earth.
e) Proud of social standing.
f) Intelligent, positive.
g) Highly intelligent, fast-thinking.
h) Musical, but weak.
i) Sensitive, engaging.
j) Ambitious, but needs security.
k) Wobbly self-esteem.
l) Determination, self-esteem.
m) Unsure of role in society.

33. a) Pretention, vulgarity.
b) This is normal in most school models. It shows balance and lack of pretention, a desire to stick to essentials.
c) Talkative, strong personality, a sense of style.

34. a) Someone who is purposeful, objective and wants to get straight to the point.
b) Indecision, ambiguity.

35. a) Overcompensating for lack of self-esteem; vanity; bravado.
b) Keen to understate one's own importance; modesty.
c) Of little significance; merely a sign that the writer signs his name many times a day.
d) Conscientiousness, fussiness.
e) Pride, self-respect.

36. a) A well-developed sense of self.
b) Shows reliability and sincerity.

37. a) More interested in himself than other people.
b) Private life is sacrificed to public life: business, or social contact.
c) Balance between private and public or social life.

38. a) Frank, open, perhaps indiscreet.
b) Sincerity.
c) Hypocritical, false.
d) Close, discreet.
e) Secretive.

39. The writer keeps people at arm's length, will go so far but no further.

40. a) Warm-hearted.
b) Sticks to essentials.

41. Scholarship or acquired intellectuality. A sense of style.

42. a) Healthy emotional appetite.
b) An interest in harmony — visual as well as emotional.
c) Vanity, sexuality.
d) Sensuality, exaggeration.
e) Sober down-to-earth personality.

43. Someone with money on his mind.

44. a) Perfectionist.
b) Thinking ahead.
c) Careful.
d) Pedantic, fussy.
e) Idealist.
f) Haste.
g) Over-emphasis on detail, eccentricity, dishonesty.
h) Spiritual, intuitive.
i) Down-to-earth, practical.
j) Unreliable.

45. a) Conventional, anxious to please.
b) Protective, warm-hearted.
c) Forward thinking.
d) Anxious to make social contact, but without emotional commitment.
e) Careful.
f) Sensitivity.
g) Determination, pig-headed.
h) Spiritual, intuitive.
i) Down-to-earth.
j) Ambitious, aggressive — especially if the stroke is sharp and pointed.
k) Pessimism.
l) Sensitivity, thought for others.
m) A good arguer, but jealous.
n) Self-protecting.
o) Protective towards others. A capacity to help others.
p) Unreliable.
q) Probably at loggerheads with a father-figure, or someone in authority.
r) Guilty conscience or inferiority.

---

25. b) Combined with long, final strokes, [**29a**] this shows a mild temperament. Combined with a high t-bar [**45h**] it shows someone with a nature which looks forward in hope.

27. d) Combined with badly formed letters this shows laziness.

29. a) If they are very long, it shows fixed opinions.

37. a) If this is combined with a leftward slant it shows a tendency to look back towards childhood. In a married woman emphasis on the Christian name shows a tendency to view herself as she was before marriage; her marriage is either not intrinsically important to her, or she is unhappy in it.

38. b) Especially sincere if the lines are straight [**1**].
d) and **e)** If either of these are combined with thick, pasty writing [**26c**], the writer is irritable, argumentative.

40. b) If simplified to the point of illegibility, this shows a thoughtless or snobbish personality.

42. e) Combined with very light pressure [**25a**] depression, dissatisfaction.

44. a) I-dots over the stem on left slanting writing indicate a good retentive memory.
c) Leftward i-dots on a left-slanting script indicate extreme caution.
e) Faint i-dots in a word which has a large first letter show shyness.
h) High i-dots with left-slanting writing [**11b**] indicate curiosity, even nosiness.

45. n) Combined with a weak stroke, lack of confidence.

The assessment of qualities

What to look for in writing—an index of characteristics

Accuracy
Very close to the school model, with some simplifications. Good rhythm. Good spacing and margins. Size of letters slightly increasing towards the end of words and lines.

Ambition
Lines sloping up. Long t-bars crossing through the stem or slanting slightly upwards.

Argumentativeness
Open 'o's and 'a's. Thick, pasty writing. Wide loops on the ascenders or t-bars slanting up.

Arrogance
Upright writing. Embellished capital letters and heavy t-bars. Embellishments in ordinary letters as well.

Brutality
Heavy pressure and thick pasty writing with emphasis on the middle zone. Left-ward trends with heavy, pointed i-dots and t-bars.

Bully
Large, impressive with heavy pressure. Narrow extension, with emphasis on the final strokes. Leftward trends, high t-bars and dagger-shaped i-dots. Triangular, sharp loops in the lower zone.

Business Ability
Small middle zone. Clearly spaced lines with neat margins. Angular or garlanded connections. Some letters like numbers.

Caution
Backward sloping writing. I-dots to the left of the stem.

Conscientiousness
Even middle zone. Straight margins and upright script. I-dots placed directly over the stems. Neat t-bars.

Cowardice
Slow, hesitant rhythm and light pressure. Narrow middle zone. Faint t-bars.

Cunning
Lines that slightly rise combined with angular connections. Uneven middle zone or a tapering middle zone. Arcaded end strokes and o's and a's open at the bottom.

Emilio Pucci
This is an elegant writing from a man who likes his riches. He is conscious of class, he is chic and he has enormous style. The 'E' in his Christian-name has two parallel lines in the centre, turning the letter into a £ sign and signifying his certainty about his aims and ambitions. The i's on their

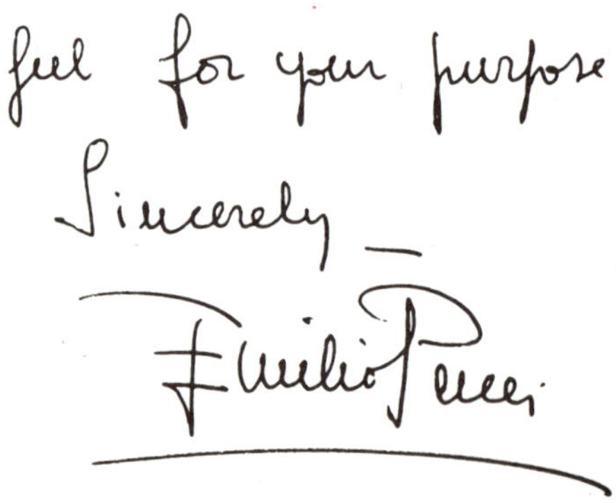

pedestals indicate pride.
This is a man who commands authority, but some of the middle zone letters spell modesty and humility. He bows to beauty.
Here, a knowledge of foreign, non-English school models is essential. This letter is typical of the Italian school model, even though it is written in English.

Deceit
Writing which slopes upwards quite steeply combined with uneven middle zone letters and a's and o's tightly knotted at the top.

Dignity
High, straight ascenders.

Dishonesty
Rising lines of small, narrow writing. Uneven middle zone letters with tight knotted a's and o's.
Slow writing. Some letters are made with several little strokes where one or two would do. 'a', 'o', 'g' and 'q' open at the bottom. A combination of arcaded and threaded connections.

Distrust
Slow but narrow writing with arcades and sometimes angled connections. Some words joined by the final strokes.

Eccentricity
Rising lines and upright writing. Small middle zone with garland connections. Embellished letters and i-dots drawn as a circle.

Egoism
Strong leftward slant. Middle zone letters larger at the beginning of words. Embellishments with angular connections in narrow writing. Tightly knotted o's and a's.

Emotional nature
Writing which slopes so far forward it almost seems to fall onto the line.

Enthusiasm
Large middle zone with writing sloping up. Heavy pressure. Emphasis on the upper zone with looped ascenders.

Exaggeration
Embellishments in large writing. Very wide margins and wide spaces between lines.

Friendliness
Garlanded connections in fully connected script. Medium sized middle zone with a definite forward movement.

Generosity
Quick, large writing with clear space between lines. Connections wide apart.

Many important qualities must be revealed in the signatures on the American Declaration of Independence!

SIGNING THE DECLARATION OF INDEPENDENCE.

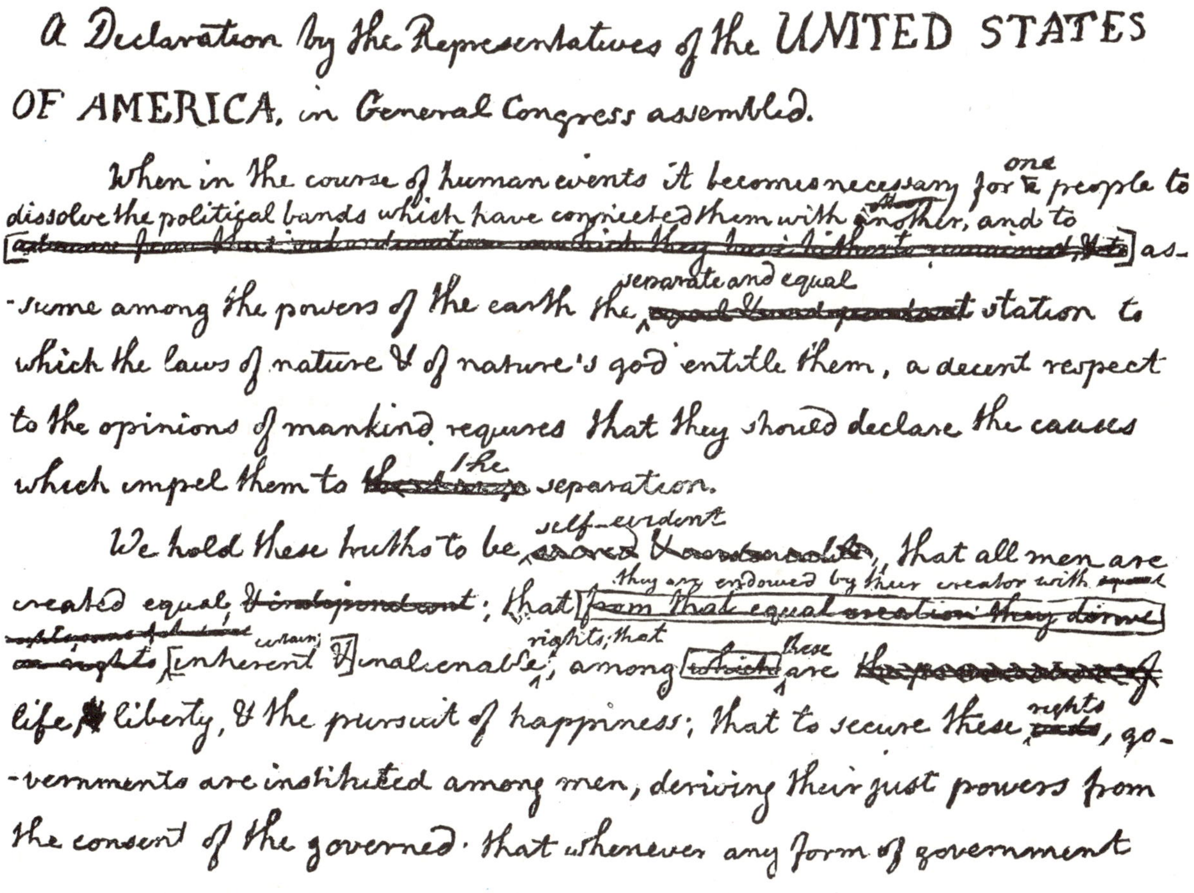

A Declaration by the Representatives of the UNITED STATES OF AMERICA, in General Congress assembled.

When in the course of human events it becomes necessary for one people to dissolve the political bands which have connected them with another, and to assume among the powers of the earth the separate and equal station to which the laws of nature & of nature's god entitle them, a decent respect to the opinions of mankind requires that they should declare the causes which impel them to the separation.

We hold these truths to be self-evident, that all men are created equal; that they are endowed by their creator with certain [inherent &] inalienable rights; that among these are life, liberty, & the pursuit of happiness; that to secure these rights, governments are instituted among men, deriving their just powers from the consent of the governed; that whenever any form of government

THE FIRST DRAFT OF THE DECLARATION OF INDEPENDENCE IN JEFFERSON'S HANDWRITING, AND WITH HIS OWN CORRECTIONS.

(From the original, preserved in Washington.)

Gentleness
Garlanded connections and light, firm pressure. Emphasis on the upper zone.

Greed
Thick, pasty writing. Large loops in the lower zone.

Honesty
Quick writing with a tendency towards the right. Garlanded connections and fine, neat spacing. Well-proportioned, no exaggerations.

Hypocrisy
Slow script. Signature smaller than the preceding text. Small a's and o's open at the bottom.

Idealism
Large but natural writing. High placed i-dots and t-bars. Emphasized upper zone, light pressure and occasional irregularities in the spacing.

The Archbishop of Westminster John, Cardinal Heenan
An erudite signature, written with soft pressure and well controlled speed. There are many scholarly formations, especially the Greek 'E'. The last letter of the signature reaches out gently for the spiritual, whilst the wavy lines, slightly ascending, show sensitivity mixed with a sense of humour. The arcaded connection

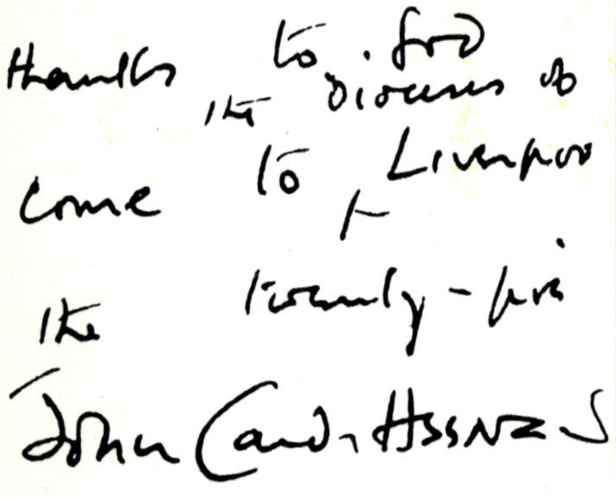

between the 'o' and 'h' in 'John' indicates the love of and adherence to tradition. Many words are woven together by large arches, his symbol of faith. Connections between words are very good, indicating free flow of thought and speech.

Inconsiderate
Irregular in shape and direction. Erratic spacing. Various connections, but with threads which impair legibility. Irregular margins.

Inferiority complex
Small but hesitant. Threaded connections; narrow extension and little pressure. Wavy lines, which also droop at the right hand margin. Neat, but narrow margins.

Intellectual balance
Fast writing with legible simplifications. Greek 'e' and 'd' formations. Good spacing and signature the same size as the rest of the handwriting.

Intuition
Quick writing with light pressure. Variability of connection including some disconnection. I-dots and t-bars connected to other letters.

Irritability
Lines sloping downwards a little. Lines rather close together. Heavy, but irregular pressure. Some signs of speed, others of slow writing. T-bars to the right of the stem.

Jealousy
Writing sloping far to the right. Final stroke of the 't' curving back to form the bar. Light pressure with some missing i-dots. Slow writing.

Kindliness
Forward sloping writing, light pressure and looped descenders and ascenders.

Logic
Letters always connected. Straight lines, small writing.

Materialism
Untidy. Heavy pressure and uneven spacing. Some pastiness and leftward tendencies. Angular connections and emphasis on the lower zone, though unpleasantly shaped.

Modesty
Tendency towards the left, with left slanting lines. Capital letters lower than the ascenders. Simple letter forms.

Opportunism
Letters tapering in size towards the end of the word. Variety of connections. Wide, but light pressure. Increasing left-hand margins.

Optimism
Fast writing with rising lines and wide script. Good spacing and large writing, but well-proportioned.
Intelligent simplifications.

Organization
Neat margins with clear spacing.
Middle zone in proportion to both upper and lower zone. Letter 'f' running from upper to lower zone.

Passion
Fast writing with extreme forward slope. Irregular pressure with pastiness. Large writing with a tendency to be narrow.

Pride
High capital letters. Embellishments. Signature larger and more embellished than normal handwriting.

Sadism
Pasty writing with emphasis on the lower zone and angular connections.
Sharply pointed final strokes. Sudden stabs of heavy pressure.

Self-confidence
Fast writing with no inconsistencies. Medium sized script with regular, firm pressure. Heavy t-bars.

Self-control
I-dots to the left of the stem in upright or forward sloping script.
Straight lines. Regularity of pressure, size and spacing.

Self-indulgence
Slow writing. Letters badly finished, tapering at the end. Capital letters slightly large.

Sensuality
Pasty writing with an extreme slant and emphasis on the lower zone.
Lack of pressure in a woman, strong pressure in a man. Clipped final strokes indicate sensuality if the writing is slow.

Sincerity
Quick, rhythmic writing, Well-spaced lines, and the extension is standard. Some simplification, but not at the expense of legibility. No leftward movement.

Talkative
Very narrow margins, almost non existent. Large writing but written very quickly. Bad spacing. Garlanded connections combined with threads.
Words joined by final strokes. Width of letters and connections and close spacing. Irregular righthand margins.

Vanity
Perfect spacing. Peculiar enrichments, but not impairing legibility. Well-proportioned middle zone but unnatural loop-formations in the lower zone. Very emphasized capital 'I'.

Religious texts were handwritten for centuries, as this medieval illumination of St Matthew indicates.

SCS MATTHEUS
EUANGELISTA.

Barbara Cartland
A full analysis

This delicately shaped writing, which shows an even finer, but firm pressure, comes from a woman who aspires to penetrate deeply into the mysteries of life. The high i-dots and ascending t-strokes show that she is determined to reach for the sky. The connection of the initial 'I' with the word 'hope' shows her determination not to let anything or anybody interfere with her plans and ideas.
The letter shapes are simple — occasionally too simple in the middle zone. The threadlike formations which result show how fast she thinks and how well she is able to concentrate on essentials. The writing is upper-zone directed. The lower zone is insignificant in both size and formation, indicating that she pursued her causes and interests not for material gain, but for the sake of propagating the ideas and ideals which have occupied her interest and imagination. The pressure indicates her determination, which uses gentle persuasion rather than domination. This does not imply that she is easily persuaded to change her ideas, as the large signature and its ascending underlining indicates. She knows what she is doing and is convinced that her causes are fair.
There is a basic gentleness and artistic sensitivity here. Look at the way the word 'Yours' is shaped. The sample was obviously written in a hurry, and the flying i-dots and t-strokes indicate that everything she undertakes is executed speedily.
The 'Yours' formation looks like a delicate flower, and people who make such shapes have a feeling for the arts. They enjoy beautiful countryside and good music.
The size of the writing contrasts sharply with the enormous signature— she feels the need to fill the page to prevent somebody else adding anything to her document. This is confirmed by her occasional over-connections, as in 'I hope' and 'my handwriting'. She is ensuring that no one else's thoughts obscure her message. After that the spacing is neat and wide, indicating that she thinks profoundly before putting her final thoughts on paper, a sign of methodical reasoning and intelligence. Some end-strokes are clipped, which is not surprising. A sensitive and intelligent person will have experienced disappointments and occasional grief, and these will have contributed to the formation of the personality which has emerged.
The size of the signature indicates pride and daring. She has to convince herself to do certain things, to try to hide her initial shyness. She hates to interfere with the privacy of others as much as she dislikes it if they meddle with her solitude.
This is a sincere, reliable and honest script from a person with ideals and ideas which she will defend with intelligent firmness and persuasion. The whole writing is intelligent rather than emotional. She has her emotions under control without suppressing them; everything is in its proper place, and in this aspect of the writing one finds a trace of old-fashioned values.

Biographical background

For most people, writing 150 books and novels, bringing up three children and running a 500 acre estate would be a full life. For Barbara Cartland these three demanding occupations are only a small part of her extraordinary life.
She embarked on her professional writing career 50 years ago as gossip columnist and soon published the first of more than one hundred romantic novels. Two years later, her first play, previously banned by the Lord Chamberlain, was performed. She was subsequently presented at Court, and, never wanting to miss the opportunity to help a friend, she wore a gown given to her by a struggling young Cambridge undergraduate, Norman Hartnell.
She participated in the General Strike of 1926, and after the birth of her first child, she organized the first of her numerous large-scale charity efforts — a pageant which she designed, produced and presented at the Albert Hall and London Pavilion.
Her two brothers were killed at Dunkirk, and she sailed with her daughter and two sons for Canada to await the end of hostilities. But when she realized that the war would be a long one, she fought for, and finally received, permission to return home. By the end of the war she was regarded as one of the nation's greatest morale boosters.
In 1955, she won the Hatfield seat on the Hertfordshire County Council and began running her 500 acre farm in a way that kept her in touch with her electorate.
Her charitable work is combined with a vigorous fight for a healthier Britain. She has campaigned, against bitter opposition, to better conditions for Nurses and Midwives and for gypsies and against fluoridation of water supplies. She has served as President of the National Health Association. She has written biographies, cookbooks, etiquette manuals and works of sociology. Now past 70, she is as

energetic as ever. Her own autobiography consists of four volumes — so far. She appears on radio and television frequently and travels thousands of miles each year, writing, lecturing and giving interviews everywhere she goes.

Key to Barbara Cartland's handwriting

[1] Reliable, conventional.
[2a] Active, positive writer who knows her aims and ambitions.
[7c] Power to concentrate; conscientious.
[8a] Another sign of a conscientious nature.
[9a] Idealism, ambition, intuition
[12] Self-control, poise; an ability to weigh up people and situations.
[13a] Practical economy.
[14a] Affectionate nature.
[17b] Well-balanced, easy-going personality.
[18c] Clear and logical.
[21d] Flexible, fast-thinking.
[22a] Spontaneity, expansiveness.
[23a] A good judge of character. A person relying partly on logic, partly on intuition.
[24c] Drive and spontaneity.
[25c] Energy, elasticity.
[27a] Spontaneity, drive action.
[29b] Reticence; disappointment.
[30b] Speed and quick thinking.
[31c] Self-respect.
[32d] Down-to-earth.
[33b] Balance; lack of pretention; a desire to stick to essentials.
[34a] Purposeful; objective; someone who wants to get straight to the point.
[35a] Lack of self-esteem.
[36b] Reliability and sincerity.
[37b] Private life sacrificed to public life.
[38d] Close, discreet.
[40a] Warm-hearted.
[44b] Thinking ahead.
[44c] Careful.
[44h] Spiritual, intuitive.
[45j] Ambitious.
[8a] and **[44a]**: painstaking.
[21d] and **[7c]**: hypersensitivity.
[22a] and **[25c]**: intuitive, ambition.

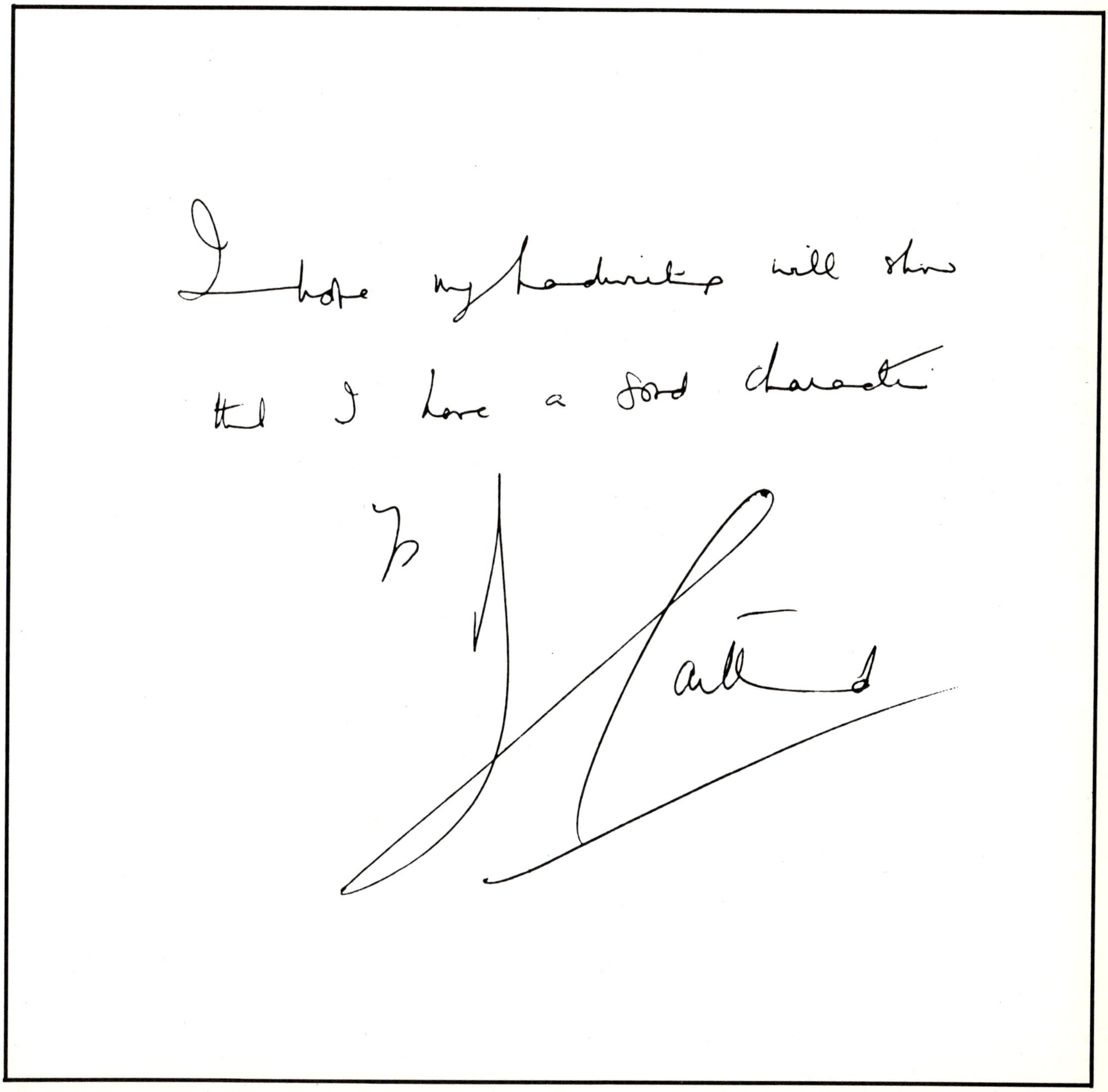

John Wayne
A full analysis

This large, speedy writing reflects an immensely active and ambitious man (look at the capital D in 'dear'). The writing is obviously derived from an American school model, but he alters it by using considerable pressure in the down-strokes. This indicates his strong sense of purpose and will to succeed. The large t-strokes also confirm this strong will. They form a kind of connection between words, eliminating any gaps in his thoughts which may be taken advantage of by others. This implies that he sees his objective clearly and that he will not permit anyone to interfere with his actions. They also show a protective nature.

The pleasant curves or garlands at the end of many words indicate that he is basically kind and generous, but the triangular loops of his 'g' and 'y' formations indicate a shrewd assessment of his chances to capitalize on situations.

The zones intermingle occasionally, but without interfering with the excellent legibility: he can combine material advantages with ambitious idealism, a rare quality which must lead to success.

His small 'a's and 'o's are carefully closed, even rolled-in, indicating that he has acquired a bit of diplomacy and is fairly tight-lipped about his plans. He has learned the hard way — the last stroke of his signature wants to keep people at a safe distance.

The last two letters of the signature gradually decrease in size showing that he has been taken for a ride more than once. He tries to prevent this from happening now, and he generally succeeds as the large lasso-loop under his name shows. The lasso reaches far to the left, as does the loop in the 'P', and some other lines have a leftward trend, such as the 't' in 'this', the 'h' in 'handwriting', and the 'e' in 'expert'. This indicates that his childhood memories are still dear to him.

Now look at the way the letters 'x' and 'p' in the word 'expert' go elegantly into all three zones. This shows an ability to organize and plan and a use of economy in fulfilling complex assignments.

The wide lefthand margin indicates that he leaves a safety-margin between himself and his objective; he is a man who thinks carefully and plans exactly before he acts. The relatively narrow righthand margin indicates that he is keen to establish contact with the outside world and anxious to please.

The general flow of this script and its large and generous size say that this man is a charming extrovert who will not let anyone influence him beyond the moral and ethical limits he has set for himself. He is almost old-fashioned in his romanticism, but shrewd enough to look after himself very satisfactorily. He is not completely without pride, as the little extra loops in the lower zone show.

He is a successful man who enjoys his achievements and admits it honestly and freely.

Biographical background

John Wayne . . . 6 foot 4 inch blue-eyed brown-haired Gemini . . . born Marion Michael Morrison, Winterset, Iowa . . . nicknamed 'Duke' as a youngster . . . moved to California in his teens . . . graduated from Glendale High School . . . scholarship grant to University of Southern California . . . worked summers at Fox Films as a 'props' man and met director John Ford . . . cast in a small role in Ford's 'Hangman's House' and went immediately back to the props dept. . . . . director Raoul Walsh call him 'John Wayne' (more appropriate for a cowboy) and gave him lead in 'The Big Trail' . . . during the Depression, he became 'Singing Sam' the screen's first musical cowboy, but couldn't sing a note . . . handed over to an unknown called Gene Autry and launched into a series of Westerns called 'Three Mesquiteers' . . . in 1939 friend John Ford cast him as the Ringo Kid in 'Stagecoach', the role which catapulted him to stardom, where he remains . . . by 1949 listed as one of ten most popular stars in the United States, where he has remained, usually in the top spot . . . in 1959 formed his own production company, Batjac, of which his son Michael is executive producer . . . produced more than a dozen films, including 'The Alamo', which he directed and starred in . . . has made more than 200 films and shows no signs of stopping . . . show business newspaper Variety calls him 'Boxoffice Champion of the World' since he has starred in 17 of the highest-earning films in movie history . . . authenticated grosses of his films have topped the 700 million dollar mark . . . in 1969 awarded the Academy Award for his role in 'True Grit', a critical and box-office success . . . seven children, four by his first marriage, and three, aged 7 to 15, by his Peruvian wife Pilar . . . now lives in Newport Bay, California, where his yacht, a converted mine sweeper christened 'The Wild Goose' can be moored a few yards away at his private pier . . . says he has no patience for golf, but he will spend hour upon hour poring over a chess board . . . plays bridge, deep-sea fishes . . . he's a devoted movie fan, who screens several films a week in his private projection room . . .

Key to John Wayne's handwriting

- [2a] Active, positive; knows his own ambitions.
- [7c] Power to concentrate, conscientiousness; critical.
- [8a] Another sign of conscientious nature.
- [9b] Idealism; ambition; intuition.
- [10a] Keenness, optimism, will to succeed.
- [13c] Desire to put a safety margin between himself and his objectives.
- [17b] This is normal; shows balanced easy-going personality.
- [18b] This is normal and shows ability to sort out ideas.
- [21a] Impressionable, receptive nature.
- [22a] Spontaneity, expansiveness.
- [24c] Drive and spontaneity.
- [25b] Energy, elasticity. This is average.
- [27a] Spontaneity, drive, action.
- [28c] Polite, conventional.
- [29d] Dogmatic attitudes.
- [30b] Speed and quick thinking.
- [31c] Self-respect.
- [33c] Talkative, strong personality, a sense of style.
- [35d] Conscientiousness.
- [35e] Pride, self-respect.
- [37c] Balance between private and public life.
- [38d] Close, discreet.
- [40a] Warm-hearted.
- [42c] Sexuality.
- [44b] Thinking ahead.
- [44f] Spiritual, intuitive.
- [45n] Self-protecting.
- [45o] Protective towards others. A capacity to help others, take them under his wing.

WARNER BROS.

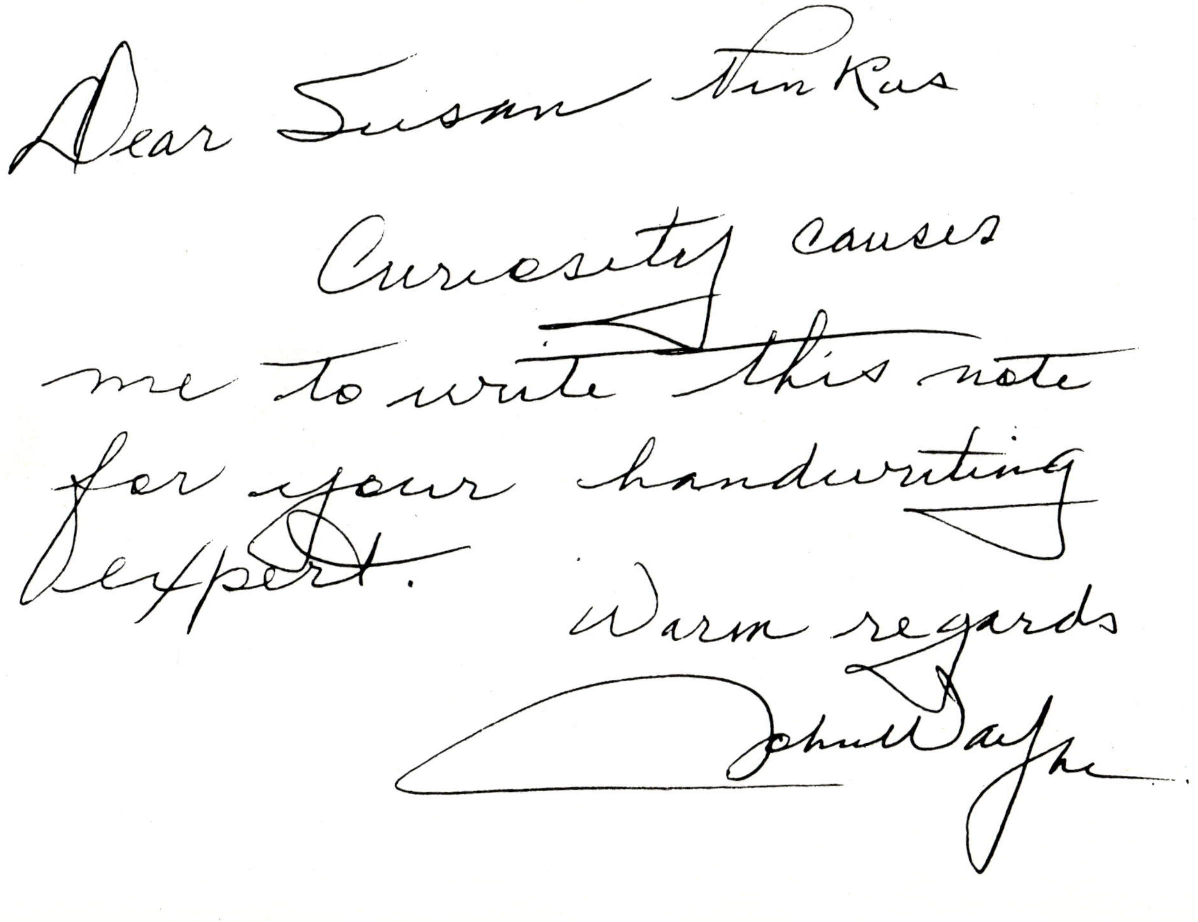

Dear Susan Pinkas

Curiosity causes me to write this note for your handwriting expert.

Warm regards

John Wayne

Writing letters

By now you will have a basic knowledge of the graphological skills and you will be able to practice them on your own or your friends' writing. Probably your first sample will be in a letter or on a postcard, though letter writing as an art seems to be going out of favour. Quite apart from the analytical possibilities, it is worth remembering that the extra effort involved is always appreciated more than the usual impersonal telephone call.

This is the age of the telephone. We use it to arrange meetings, to keep in touch with those we love, to announce our good and bad news. We call one another up to gossip, to settle arguments, to quarrel, to make up, to offer comfort, to express love. However, the telephone has not always dominated our lives in this way. As little as 20 or 30 years ago, people would write letters whenever they felt the need for contact with their friends and relatives.

Parted lovers undoubtedly used the telephone occasionally, but they softened the pain of absence with letters which expressed their deepest feelings for each other. Husbands and wives who were parted wrote to each other. Grown-up children sent news home regularly. Families remained in touch and closely-knit through the letters they exchanged and friendships were kept alive for decades.

There are many rewards to letter-writing. Letters link those who are parted and keep friendships alive and meaningful. They also allow us to enter into really close relationships with our special friends. It is often much easier to express innermost thoughts and feelings in a letter than in person. Letters, because they give the reader time and privacy to react, can also be used to ease a difficult situation; to break news gently; to explain awkward events tactfully; to mend quarrels gracefully.

Perhaps the greatest value of letters is that they give lasting pleasure. The amusing telephone call from a girl-friend is over as soon as the receiver is replaced.

Letters should give great pleasure to both the writer and the recipient. Try to think of letter-writing as an art and not as a chore.

Half an hour later it will be hard to remember three phrases from the conversation. A quick telephone call will give lovers instant togetherness, but this sense of nearness vanishes as swiftly as it came. Letters provide a lasting record of the significant moments in life. Like entries in a diary, they have the power to conjure up vividly the situation which existed at the time they were written.

Letters can be broadly grouped into four categories: formal letters; social letters; letters to close friends; and love letters.

Even the most reluctant letter-writer will not always be able to avoid writing formal letters from time to time. These are the letters which have to be written to total strangers: when applying for a job, returning a completed income-tax form or making a hotel reservation.

The essential thing about these letters is that they should be clear, brief and strictly to the point. The letter to the hotel, for example, must specify the date for which the reservation is being made, the number of rooms required, and any other details such as whether the room is to have twin beds or a double. Unnecessary information should be omitted as the reservations clerk will have countless letters to process.

Letters applying for jobs fall into a slightly more sensitive area, for here a hint of personality can be allowed to creep in, to distinguish one application from another. But this is dangerous territory and, strictly speaking, letters have to do two things only: express the candidate's interest in and enthusiasm for the job in question, and outline the qualifications and experience that make him or her suitable for the post.

Letters of application must be organized to convey the necessary information in the clearest possible way. Employers tend to be busy people and may impatiently dismiss a rambling letter. The director of a marketing company will not be at all interested in the fact that his prospective secretary is a brilliant needlewoman. But the fact that she speaks French, although the advertisement for the job may have made no mention of languages, will attract his attention. A talent for needlework would, however, be

worth mentioning if the vacancy were in the office of a school of embroidery design, as it would give the candidate a clear advantage over the others.

A useful way of applying for a job when there is a lot of information to convey is to send in a typed curriculum vitae [resumé] which gives details of age, sex, education, qualifications, employment, spare-time occupations, and anything else that could interest a prospective employer. This should be accompanied by a short, handwritten, letter which expresses interest in the vacancy and perhaps draws attention to the most relevant achievements. Jobs for which one has to fill in a printed application form should be returned with a similar letter.

When a hint of individuality can be introduced into a letter for a job without sounding coy, flippant, or slick, so much the better. But this should always be done with the very greatest of care, for it is of secondary importance to clarity and conciseness and can often misfire. If in doubt it is far better to limit the letter to straight facts expressed in as natural a way as possible.

Even the most impersonal letters to strangers can be formal in tone without sounding stilted. There are, however, fairly strict conventions governing the style of address and endings of formal letters which, although not really complicated, can be difficult to negotiate without a little practice.

Very formal letters open with the words 'Dear Sir' or 'Dear Madam' and end 'Yours faithfully' or 'Yours truly'. Some very staid institutions continue to address their correspondents in this way long after they know their names, but this is becoming increasingly unusual. Normally, as the correspondence progresses, 'Dear Sir' very soon becomes 'Dear Mr Smith', and then perhaps 'Dear Charles'. 'Yours faithfully' leaves the scene a fraction earlier than 'Yours truly', giving way to 'Yours sincerely' 'Yours ever', or just 'Yours'. So the least formal letter will begin with 'Dear Charles' and end 'Yours ever' or 'Yours'.

In formal letters each ritual step from one stage to the next is an unspoken acknowledgement on both sides that the relationship is moving away from formality towards near-friendship. If you are unsure about changing to a less formal style, take your cue from your correspondent. If he bypasses the 'Dear Sir', 'Yours faithfully' stage altogether and plunges in with 'Dear Mr Jones', 'Yours sincerely' from the beginning, do the same; when he starts addressing you by your christian name, address him by his. If you do not you may unintentionally offend him. Addressing someone as 'Dear Mr Smith' when he has written 'Dear John' to you can be interpreted as a signal that you think he is being over-familiar and wish to restore the correspondence to its earlier formality. The only exception to this is when there is a great disparity in age or status, as, for example, in the employer-employee relationship, when the employee may feel that it is more respectful to continue to use the more formal 'Dear Mr Brown', although she herself may be being addressed as 'Dear Jane'.

Simple, everyday language will always convey your message best, whatever the content. Try to write naturally and briefly even in a formal letter.

Party invitations come into the category of formal correspondence. They are usually specially printed and follow the format 'John Smith requests the pleasure of the company of Jane Brown at his 21st birthday party'. Until recently the convention was that you should reply to such an invitation with corresponding formality, no matter how well you knew the sender. So Jane Brown would reply 'Jane Brown thanks Mr John Smith for his kind invitation which she is very pleased to accept'. This still remains the correct way to answer such an invitation, but in the relaxed social climate of today, many people find this artificially rather embarrassing. Except for very formal functions and replies to hostesses who might be offended by a casual approach, it is now accepted that the response to these invitations may be in a more informal vein.

Two further points are worth remembering about formal letters. First, always quote the date and reference number of any earlier correspondence – large firms have very complex filing systems. Secondly, avoid business jargon such as 'Referring to yours of 7th inst' or 'the 12th ult'. It is unnecessary, ugly and old-fashioned. Simple, everyday language is more attractive.

Social letters range from short thank-you notes for presents or hospitality to long epistles sending news to your grandmother. The easy, relaxed letters which fall into this category are letters to enjoy. They have none of the difficult style points encountered in formal letters. Friends can be addressed in any way and any conventional, quirky or affectionate ending can be used.

Style in social letters, in so far as it exists at all, is a simple question of suiting the tone of the letter to the degree of friendship involved, so that what is written is appropriate to both the person and the occasion. They can be as lively and interesting as can be managed without sounding contrived.

Common politeness makes some social letters more or less obligatory. Letters of thanks, congratulations and condolence fall into this category. In many cases the correspondents may not know each other very well, but it should be possible to convey some feeling without being hypocritical. Write naturally, briefly and sincerely rather than at length. (The recipient can often tell when the writer has struggled to think of something with which to fill the page.) A good social letter should make the recipient feel that their gift or hospitality has really been appreciated, or their loss or success, genuinely acknowledged. A friendly, lively, communication should really brighten the recipient's day. In time the writing of such letters can become an art in itself, giving enormous pleasure not only to those who receive them, but to their writers too.

Letters to close friends are everything letters to more casual friends are, but they convey deeper feelings. There are no rules for composing them except to write with the same warmth, naturalness, and lack of inhibition which would be shown in a face-to-face situation. Letters like these simply provide a means of sharing the highs and lows of every-day life with friends who are absent. They can be written on many different levels but, with real trust on both sides, communication by letter can be a very enriching experience.

Love-letters will be the most treasured letters of all. They have to make up for separation. Because they will be read as if the writer were present, they should be written warmly and tenderly. Above all, a lover should respond to the other's warmth and love. Nothing is more hurtful than a correspondence between lovers in which one is tender and forthcoming and the other reserved and cool. Indifference in love-letters can damage a relationship more surely than any word of anger spoken during a personal exchange for the writer will not be there to put things right with a look or a touch. Sensitively written, however, love-letters can be the next best thing to being together. They can lead lovers to an even better understanding of each other and bring them closer on all sorts of levels, from shared jokes to deep thoughts and feelings.

Whatever its purpose, a letter is a personal and lasting way of communicating. And while people continue to enjoy writing to each other, the art of letter-writing will not disappear.

Doodles

The previous pages have shown you how to analyze handwriting: but there is another form of writing well worth considering which in very many instances appears more like drawing: the doodle.

It may prove surprising but doodles — freely-drawn Freudian slips of the pen that they are — often come straight from your subconscious: that part of the mind which in all of us consists of a wealth of unadmitted desires, inhibitions and fears and which lies hidden far behind the public mask we all wear. As such, they are not as trivial as most people mistakenly believe, but often all-important clues to personality.

Most of us doodle. Research has proved this: so that those who are quick to deny that they ever do have probably always ignored their doodles in the past or completely destroyed the evidence. Patterns vary enormously, but most of us tend to have one particular design which we repeatedly put on paper, whatever variations on the basic theme we may sometimes employ. Women, for instance, most commonly doodle flowers and leaves: hardly surprising when one considers the obvious feminine symbolism of 'coming into bloom'. On the other hand, boxes — and three-dimensional figures generally — are more masculine doodles, though this is not to say that they are never drawn by women. Series of straight lines and boxes which have obviously been built in an upward formation are usually pointers to methodical, logical thinkers. Houses, adolescent film-star-type facial doodles and hearts either cruelly pierced with an arrow or lavishly bound with satin ribbon are obviously idealistic, wish-fulfilment doodles — doodles that show a marked subconscious desire for glamour, love and security. Many more abstract patterns are taken up simply because they are satisfying shapes to draw, since repetitive even strokes are required. They are often 'S' shapes, with the treble clef and snail shapes by far the most popular.

Some people find it equally pleasing to fill in open letters in newspaper headlines or in advertisement copy. They are probably not particularly original or creative, but excel when working within a given structure or framework, operate well in a team and follow orders and instructions admirably.

The size of doodles and the intensity of ink or pencil lead while doodling are, as with handwriting, often indicative of the emotional state at the time of doodling. Spot a repeatedly scored-through doodle, dark and uneven, and it is likely to have been penned in anger. Softer, more 'open' doodles suggest a happier frame of mind and perhaps a more easy-going temperament. But investigators have found that large, dynamic doodles are not always the doodles of out-and-out extroverts, Large doodles taking up a vast amount of space on a clean sheet of paper are often habitually drawn by the introverted, shy and retiring personality who really desires to be more outward-going in company, regrets his of her inability to be sociable and who resorts to displacing a repressed largeness of personality on to paper. Those doodles which you find yourself scribbling while on the telephone or listening to the radio can in fact tell you an enormous amount about yourself. And the information you glean should in turn, if used wisely, help you to fathom much of the iceberg — the real, underlying you. Study the doodles of family, friends and colleagues, too, as you find them lurking in notepads or on blotting paper. A doodle will, of course, never provide total personality analysis; but it could be a step towards greater understanding and thus an enrichment of relationships.

Search your notepad and you're sure to find one of these common types of doodle! Clockwise: flowers, spirals, s-shapes, animals, patterns, boxes.